Blender 3D Printing Essentials

Bring your ideas to life in Blender and learn how to design beautiful, light, and strong 3D printed objects

Gordon Fisher

[PACKT] open source *
PUBLISHING   community experience distilled

BIRMINGHAM - MUMBAI

About the Author

Gordon Fisher, as a teenager, studied drafting and built plastic model cars. He got his start in 3D computer modeling back when one would have to create a 3D engineering drawing with a pencil and then input the information into a computer, vertex-by-vertex.

He led a three-person crew in building 3D models of 80 aircraft for the U.S. Army Visual Aircraft Recognition program. He also built an accurate model of the 17th and 18th holes of the Pebble Beach golf course for Callaway Golf's golf simulator. He's currently working with the Open Luna Foundation to create models, X3D and 3D printed, of their parts of their proposed lunar base.

He is the Creative Director at Point Happy Interactive. He has been using Blender professionally since 2002 and has given classes on using Blender and using Python with Blender at Python conferences in Texas and Arkansas. His work has been displayed at the National Air and Space Museum. He is also the author of the book *Blender 3D Basics*, published by Packt Publishing.

I would like to thank all the people who helped me write this book, especially Subho Gupta, the Commissioning Editor, and Amey Sawant, the Project Coordinator. I'd also like to thank Bart Veldhuisen of Blender Nation and Shapeways and Gary Fudge of mCor Technologies for taking the time to answer all my questions, and all the people who have devoted so many hours to developing better and less expensive 3D printers.

About the Reviewers

Sandra Gilbert started using Blender in the fall of 2000. Back then, there were not as many tutorials or educational resources available for Blender artists, so she, like many others, figured it out as she went along. Over the years, Sandra has seen not only Blender, but the community itself grow and mature. Now, there is a wealth of tutorials and educational materials available.

She is the Managing Editor of Blenderart Magazine. In 2005, she and her friend, Gaurav Nawani, decided to start Blenderart Magazine. Blenderart Magazine is a theme-based community magazine offering Blender tutorials, interviews, and making of articles.

Having been part of such a large open source community and watching how the community comes together to create and accomplish large projects, she knows that Blenderart's success is due in large part to the Blender community itself. The community supports their endeavor in many ways, the biggest being by contributing articles, tutorials, and images to be published in each issue.

I would like to thank all the talented writers and educators in the Blender community for sharing their knowledge and helping in teaching a new generation of Blender users.

Taylor Petrick is currently a student at the University of Waterloo in Canada. He took an interest in 3D graphics and modeling in middle school and has continued to develop his skills ever since. He has a strong programming background, with over six years of practical experience using C++ and technologies such as OpenGL, DirectX, and CUDA. Currently, he is working with ray tracing and investigating its potential for use in real-time applications.

He uses Blender3D both as a tool for his projects and to create artwork as a hobby. He first started using Blender to make models and animations for a video game project and has actively used it ever since. He is excited about 3D printing and how quickly it is entering widespread use. He is particularly interested in the Peachy Printer, a new low-cost option that interfaces directly with Blender.

I'd like to thank Packt for giving me the opportunity to be involved in the review process of this book. It was the first time I had a chance to work on such a project and I was fortunate enough to be chosen as a technical reviewer. Sharing knowledge has always been important to me, so I was glad to contribute my skills to help others learn. I enjoyed working with the team and becoming more familiar with the review process in general.

www.PacktPub.com

Support files, eBooks, discount offers and more

You might want to visit www.PacktPub.com for support files and downloads related to your book.

Did you know that Packt offers eBook versions of every book published, with PDF and ePub files available? You can upgrade to the eBook version at www.PacktPub.com and as a print book customer, you are entitled to a discount on the eBook copy. Get in touch with us at service@packtpub.com for more details.

At www.PacktPub.com, you can also read a collection of free technical articles, sign up for a range of free newsletters and receive exclusive discounts and offers on Packt books and eBooks.

http://PacktLib.PacktPub.com

Do you need instant solutions to your IT questions? PacktLib is Packt's online digital book library. Here, you can access, read and search across Packt's entire library of books.

Why Subscribe?

*   Fully searchable across every book published by Packt
*   Copy and paste, print and bookmark content
*   On demand and accessible via web browser

Free Access for Packt account holders

If you have an account with Packt at www.PacktPub.com, you can use this to access PacktLib today and view nine entirely free books. Simply use your login credentials for immediate access.

Building texture maps   28
  Choosing colors for printing   28
  UV unwrapping   29
Painting the texture map   40
  Exporting the UV Layout for use in an external paint program   40
  Painting your texture in Blender   40
Summary   **43**

Chapter 3: Making a Blender Model that's Ready to Print   **45**
What is special about 3D printing?   **45**
Installing the Print3D toolbox   **46**
Introducing the Print3D toolbox   **47**
Introducing the Mesh Analysis panel   **47**
Setting up the units of the scene   **48**
Making a 3D model that will print   **49**
Making a watertight model   49
Making a manifold model   50
  Inspecting objects to see if they are manifold or non-manifold   51
  Finding problems that make a file non-manifold   52
Fixing noncontiguous edges   53
Typical problem areas with a model   **55**
Fixing distorted polygons   55
Blunting sharp edges   59
Fixing the junction between blade and hilt   63
Economizing when 3D printing   **64**
Summary   **65**

Chapter 4: Making Strong, Light Objects with the Solidify Modifier   **67**
Optimizing wall thickness   **67**
Using Solidify for proper wall thickness   **68**
Analyzing and modifying the inner shell   69
Making the dragon useful   **77**
Cutting holes for removing extra printing material   79
Precision modeling—fitting two objects together   81
Dealing with overhangs and support   82
  If the printer automatically makes supports   83
  Making supports for your model   83
Exporting your 3D object   **85**
Getting the orientation right   86
Making an STL file   86
Making an X3D file with a texture   87
Summary   **88**

Appendix: 3D Printing References   **89**

References   **89**
3D printing services   90
3D printers – hobbyist   90
3D printers – industrial   91
3D objects   92

Index   **93**

Preface

You know that 3D printing is hot. You wouldn't have bought this book if you didn't. What I hope you will get from this book is an introduction to building a model in Blender so it will make a good object in a 3D printer.

This is fairly simple. Mostly, you need to know what information the 3D printer needs to make an object, what considerations you need to make when designing your object, and which techniques you can use to achieve your goals.

I have tried to avoid being printer-specific. 3D printing is in the phase where new printers are appearing every day. At some point, there will be a shakeout where the best printer makers prevail, but it's too early to guess which companies those will be. But among all kinds of printers, there are basic rules that will work with any printer, and you will learn how to tailor your objects for particular printers.

While I have worked to ensure that you could do each step demonstrated, I assume that you have a general knowledge of operating Blender, such as one would get from my book *Blender 3D Basics*, also available on the Packt website.

Let's get started!

What this book covers

Chapter 1, *Designing Objects for 3D Printing*, gives you a glimpse into the general issues affecting 3D printing and background on what is going on, so you understand why you may have to do things differently to make an object in Blender for 3D printing than you do for animation or the game engine.

Chapter 2, *Measuring and Texturing Techniques for 3D Printing*, explains how to prepare a file to be used in 3D printing. We will cover using the Ruler/Protractor tool to measure objects and some methods used in texturing the model.

Chapter 3, Making a Blender Model that's Ready to Print, explains how to make models that are watertight, manifold, and will print well.

Chapter 4, Making Strong, Light Objects with the Solidify Modifier, explains how to make an object strong and light using the Solidify modifier and how to clean up the model. You will also learn about doing precision modeling, dealing with overhangs, and finally you will learn how to export the completed file.

Appendix, contains links to good background material on 3D printing, 3D printing services, hobbyist-level 3D printers, industrial-level 3D printers, and Blender objects available on the web.

What you need for this book

Blender 2.67 or higher and a general understanding of standard modeling techniques, such as described in *Blender 3D Basics*.

Who this book is for

People who want to be able to build 3D printed objects using Blender to model the object(s).

Conventions

In this book, you will find a number of styles of text that distinguish between different kinds of information. Here are some examples of these styles, and an explanation of their meaning.

Code words in text are shown as follows: "Set the radius of the brush to about 25 and the strength to 1.0".

New terms and **important words** are shown in bold. Words that you see on the screen, in menus or dialog boxes for example, appear in the text like this: "In the **UV/ Image Editor** header, select **Image**".

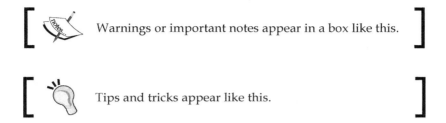

Warnings or important notes appear in a box like this.

Tips and tricks appear like this.

Reader feedback

Feedback from our readers is always welcome. Let us know what you think about this book—what you liked or may have disliked. Reader feedback is important for us to develop titles that you really get the most out of.

To send us general feedback, simply send an e-mail to feedback@packtpub.com, and mention the book title via the subject of your message. If there is a topic that you have expertise in and you are interested in either writing or contributing to a book, see our author guide on www.packtpub.com/authors.

Customer support

Now that you are the proud owner of a Packt book, we have a number of things to help you to get the most from your purchase.

Downloading the example code

You can download the example code files for all Packt books you have purchased from your account at http://www.packtpub.com. If you purchased this book elsewhere, you can visit http://www.packtpub.com/support and register to have the files e-mailed directly to you.

Downloading the color images of this book

We also provide you a PDF file that has color images of the screenshots/diagrams used in this book. The color images will help you better understand the changes in the output. You can download this file from http://www.packtpub.com/sites/default/files/downloads/4597OS_ColoredGraphics.pdf

Errata

Although we have taken every care to ensure the accuracy of our content, mistakes do happen. If you find a mistake in one of our books—maybe a mistake in the text or the code—we would be grateful if you would report this to us. By doing so, you can save other readers from frustration and help us improve subsequent versions of this book. If you find any errata, please report them by visiting http://www.packtpub.com/submit-errata, selecting your book, clicking on the **errata submission form** link, and entering the details of your errata. Once your errata are verified, your submission will be accepted and the errata will be uploaded on our website, or added to any list of existing errata, under the Errata section of that title. Any existing errata can be viewed by selecting your title from http://www.packtpub.com/support.

Piracy

Piracy of copyright material on the Internet is an ongoing problem across all media. At Packt, we take the protection of our copyright and licenses very seriously. If you come across any illegal copies of our works, in any form, on the Internet, please provide us with the location address or website name immediately so that we can pursue a remedy.

Please contact us at copyright@packtpub.com with a link to the suspected pirated material.

We appreciate your help in protecting our authors, and our ability to bring you valuable content.

Questions

You can contact us at questions@packtpub.com if you are having a problem with any aspect of the book, and we will do our best to address it.

1
Designing Objects for 3D Printing

3D printing! It's big, it's exciting, and it's fun! It's so important that Microsoft made being 3D printing compatible a high priority for Windows 8.1. This book will help you get started in using Blender to make objects specifically for 3D printing. We will not recommend any particular printer or printing service. If you already have a 3D printer, you will know what you need to do for printing. If not, you'll probably be depending on someone else to do the actual printing and you'll need to know what they need from you, and what you need to keep in mind as you model in Blender.

In this chapter, we will look into general issues affecting 3D printing and give you a little background on what is going on so you understand why you may have to do things differently to make an object in Blender for 3D printing than you do for animation or a game engine.

The following are the topics we'll be covering in this chapter:

- Opportunities to use your 3D printer
- How a 3D printer works
- Modeling dimensions, tolerances, and file sizes
- Controlling printing costs
- What materials can I use in 3D printing?
- What types of printers are there?
- A tour of a 3D printing service

Opportunities to use your 3D printer

3D printing is not the correct way to make everything. If you need to make a lot of copies of an object, 3D printing is too slow. 3D printing is also expensive. You have a limited choice of materials. You have limits on the size of objects and the quality of the objects you can make.

For example, think about making a bicycle completely with 3D printing. While I am writing this, it's impossible. The tires alone are impossible, with rubber, thread, and steel cords; the process is too complex for today's 3D printers. The size of the bike frame is still too large for almost all 3D printers; carbon fiber frames cannot be printed directly, titanium frames are very expensive, and the quality of steel you would be able to use in a 3D printer may not be right for a durable bike.

At the same time, you could easily make custom lugs to hold the frame together, custom light mounts, shifters, and water bottle racks. 3D printing can be used to create the mold for carbon fiber lugs or even a mold for a carbon fiber frame.

3D printing is best used for making prototypes and custom objects. As an exercise, I looked around to see what kinds of things I'd want to use 3D printing for. I came up with the following things:

- Water bottle holder for my recumbent bicycle's oval-shaped frame
- A clip that would let me mount my hydration pack to my recumbent bike and hold the hose securely next to my shirt, yet be convenient to move so I can drink from it, and it detaches easily in case of an accident
- Replacement for the plastic table clamp of an old Luxo lamp
- Replacement plastic foot for a camera tripod
- Extension for my mouse to make it large enough for my hand
- 3D-printed business cards
- Z-shaped key for an antique Chinese brass lock that had accidentally got latched, and for which there was no key. As seen in the following image, the new key was simple to make in 3D printing but difficult to make otherwise:

I'm sure that you have your own list. The great part about 3D printers is that they can make any shape you need, and they do it in a reasonable time at a reasonable cost. That's amazingly powerful. Look at the catalogs of the services linked later if you need more ideas.

You may want to use 3D printing as a part of a business. You could make prototypes of mechanical parts and objects architectural or theatrical stage models. You can sell what you make, such as jewelry, fantasy figurines, a smart phone case, custom coffee cups or vases, cookie molds in the shape of a cat, or whatever you think of.

3D printing is just getting started, so there is no telling how far it will go. A company named Made in Space is designing a 3D printer for use in zero gravity. They see that it will be far more efficient for many space-based repairs to just make parts up there, rather than having to carry a large number of spare parts into orbit. The OpenLuna Foundation is using 3D printing to build a model of their proposed lunar lander to show potential investors. Being able to touch and hold something is a powerful influencer in making a sale:

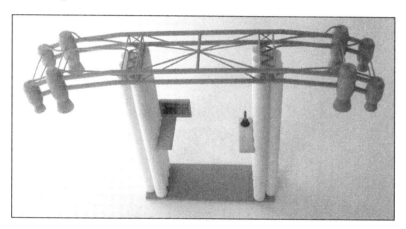

How a 3D printer works

A 3D printer needs to take a description of a three-dimensional object and turn it into a physical object. Like Blender, a 3D printer uses values along the X, Y, and Z axes to determine the shape of an object. But where Blender sees an object as perhaps cylinders, spheres, cubes, or edges and faces, a 3D printer is all about layers and perimeters.

First, a **slicing program** opens the object file that you made and it slices the object into vertical layers as seen in the following screenshot:

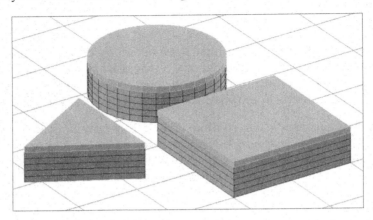

Then, each layer is printed out one by one in a growing stack as seen in the following screenshot:

But you can get a better idea of how these layers stack up if you can see it interactively. I have provided an interactive illustration that allows you to see the dragon slice by slice. Scrolling through the frames, you can see how the walls of the dragon's body are built:

1. Open up `45970S_01_LayersDisplay.blend` in your download packet. Examine the thickness of the body at each layer.

2. Press *Alt* + *A* to play the animation. Press *Esc* to stop playing it.

3. You can also drag the current time indicator in the timeline back and forth to look at individual frames, or use the right and left arrow keys.

Note how the dragon starts as a series of islands. Look at the dragon's hands. The fingers start off floating in space until they are joined to the arms.

The exact method a 3D printer uses to print a layer varies. Some printers work like a pencil, drawing an outline of the shape on that layer and then filling in the shape with cross-hatching. Look at the left side of the preceding screenshot again.

The printer would first outline the tail, then fill it in. Next, it would move to one haunch, outline it, and fill it in, and then the other. And finally, it would outline and fill each foot. You can get a better idea of how this happens with this 3D printer's **hot end** simulator. The hot end is the printer's nozzle where the 3D printing material is extruded.

> Open `4597_01_HotEnd.blend` and follow the instructions shown there.

Other printers may use a print head much like an inkjet printer. The print head moves across the printing bed and deposits material where needed.

> **Downloading the example code**
>
> You can download the example code files for all Packt books you have purchased from your account at `http://www.packtpub.com`. If you purchased this book elsewhere, you can visit `http://www.packtpub.com/support` and register to have the files e-mailed directly to you.

Types of 3D printers

So what kinds of printers are there? How do they print and how are they different? The terminology is still a bit confusing. The **American Society for Testing and Materials (ASTM International)** recently came up with the following categories:

- **Material extrusion** is also known as **Molten Polymer Deposition (MPD)**, **Fused Deposition Modeling (FDM)**, or **Fused Filament Fabrication (FFF)**; these extrude a gooey material out in layers to build up the proper shape. This is the class of printers that includes most hobbyist 3D printers. They work like the simulator you just used. These can use plastic, metal wire, wax, sugar, frosting, chocolate, cookie dough pasta, pizza, and even corn chips.

- **Material jetting** is also known as **photopolymer jetting**. Like an inkjet, this printer squirts liquid photopolymers at the right moment, which are cured immediately with ultraviolet light, layer by layer. The object being built is supported by a layer of gel that is also applied by the print head, so overhang is not a problem.

- **Binder jetting** uses a two part system. A thin layer of composite material is spread across the print bed. Then, an inkjet-like printing head sprays a binder fluid and possibly colored ink, which combine with the composite material to produce solid colored and sometimes textured objects. This can be plastic, gypsum, or metals, such as copper, tungsten, bronze, and stainless steel. For metals, a second step is needed to make them solid. The binder is removed and metal is infused where the binder used to be.

- **Sheet lamination printers** may use materials, such as paper or metal, and will color, cut out, and glue layers together into objects.

- **Vat photopolymerization** is also called **Stereolithography (SLA)**. Photopolymerization printers use light to cure liquid material into the right shape. This process uses resins, wax, or liquid plastics for the material. It may use a laser or a high resolution DLP video projector similar to one you would hook up to your computer to give a PowerPoint presentation.

- **Powder bed fusion** is also known as **Granular Materials Binding**. These printers use a laser or heat to fuse layers of powder into the right shape. These can use metal, ceramic, gypsum, or plastic powder. There are several subtypes of powder bed fusion printers.

- **Selective Laser Sintering (SLS)** is used with thermoplastics, wax, and ceramic powders. A thin coat of powder is spread across the printing bed. Then, the printing head prints the layer by fusing selected areas with the laser. The printing bed then drops down. Another coat of powder is added and the laser prints the next layer.

- **Selective heat sintering (SHS)** uses heat instead of a laser and can be used with thermoplastic powder.

- **Direct Metal Laser Sintering (DMLS)** or **Selective Laser Melting (SLM)** is a subcategory of selective laser sintering. The laser beam melts the metal and makes solid parts with metal alloys like aluminum, iron, stainless steel, maraging steel, nickel, chromium, cobalt, and titanium alloys. In theory, it can be used with most alloys.

- **Directed energy deposition**, also known as **Electron Beam Melting (EBM)**, is similar to SLS, but uses an electron beam instead of a laser. The high heat generated by the electron beam allows use of pure metal powder such as titanium alloys, and can make high-detail, high-strength objects that do not need any postmanufacturing heat treatment.

Question: Earlier, I mentioned a company named Made In Space, which is making a 3D printer to be used in zero gravity. What kind of printer is it making?

1. Directed energy deposition
2. Vat photopolymerization
3. Material extrusion
4. Powder bed fusion

Answer: Option 3, material extrusion is correct. Extruding a material avoids liquid or powder floating around in zero gravity.

Basic parts of a 3D printer

As you have observed, there are a wide variety of 3D printers. But there are some parts they all have in common.

The printing bed is what the 3D object is built upon.

The printing head holds the laser, the printing jet, or the hot end of the extruder.

And then there are controls to position the printing bed and the printing head in relation to each other; one control for the X dimension, one for the Y dimension, and one for the Z dimension.

There are no hard and fast rules for which controls the printing bed and printing head have. The **Cube** printing head is controlled in the X dimension only and the printing bed is controlled in the Y and Z dimensions, whereas the **MendelMaxPro** puts X and Z controls on the printer head and controls the printing bed only in the Y dimension.

How is a 3D printer controlled?

Generally, the answer is **stepper motors**. Stepper motors are motors that move in small discrete angles of rotation instead of spinning like most regular motors. This allows you to make definite, easily repeatable motions. It is also one reason why there are minimum sizes on the detail that you can make. A 3D printer can't make detail smaller than one step of the stepper motor.

Then, through wires, drums, gears, and threaded rods, the motion of the stepper motor is scaled to fit the medium that the printer uses. A hobbyist printer that uses a filament of the ABS or PLA plastic that feeds off of a reel will provide the kind of detail that those plastics can support. A high-end stereolithography printer may get much finer detail.

The next graphic is a diagram of the insides of a stepper motor. The rotor is in the center. It rotates and is attached to a shaft that pokes out of the motor. The stators are attached to the outer shell of the motor. They are wrapped with copper wire and an electrical current is run through the wire to give each stator a negative charge, a positive charge, or no charge as indicated in the next graphic. In the graphic, red represents a positive charge, the blue is a negative charge, and the grey has no charge.

The rotor in the center has 50 teeth. The stators around the outside have a total of 48 teeth. It's this imbalance in the number of teeth that allow the stepper motor's rotor to walk around step-by-step.

The positive charge of the rotor is attracted to the stator teeth that are negatively charged. In the following screenshot, you can see that the rotor teeth aren't well aligned with the uncharged stator that is counter-clockwise from the blue stator. To do a single step, the stepper motor controller changes the negative charge from the blue stator in the following screenshot to the stator just counter-clockwise to it. Then, the teeth in the rotor try to align with that stator. So, the rotor moves just a little, a step. To continue moving more steps, the stator with the negative charge keeps moving to the next stator, as follows:

 To see how this works, open the interactive 4597_01_ StepperDemo.blend file and follow the instructions.

- Shop around for a printer who charges less.
- Use a less expensive material.
- Make your object smaller.
- Hollow out your object.
- Remove unneeded material, in the lunar lander, the fuel tank clusters were built as a single hollow object instead of individual tanks. The landing pad is not a solid block; underneath, it's like an upside down soda crate. The rocket motors are not solid.
- Delete unneeded details.

Materials for 3D printing

There are hundreds of materials used in 3D printing, such as plastics, ceramics, metal, and food. Here are some of the more common materials.

Acrylonitrile Butadiene Styrene (ABS) is currently the most popular plastic for 3D printing. It is lightweight, shiny, easily extruded, strong, impact resistant, and heat tolerant. It's used for the interiors of cars, household appliances, and more. It requires high heat to extrude. While being extruded, it does give off fumes, so the printer should be in a well-ventilated room. ABS is not generally recycled.

Polylactic acid (PLA) is made from lactic acid, the same chemical that builds up in your muscles when you exercise hard. PLA melts at a lower temperature than ABS. The PLA objects are stronger and take wear better than ABS. PLA is used for things, such as plastic cups, fabric, and microwave trays. PLA is derived from natural sources, such as corn starch, tapioca roots, or sugar cane. It is recyclable.

Aliphatic polyamide (nylon) is a family of materials. Invented as a synthetic silk, some early uses were in ladies stockings and parachutes. Nylon is cheap, tough, flexible, and can be dyed. Nylon is less brittle than ABS and PLA, so it can take a beating. It's also somewhat self-lubricating, which is good for making gears. But nylon is also more prone to warping, and is stringier when printing than ABS or PLA. Nylon is recyclable.

Polyethylene terephthalate (PET), also known as Dacron or polyester, is often used for soda and water bottles because the plastic's chemicals don't leak into the food. It is strong and it takes a lot of wear, so it's used for recording and adhesive tape as well as "space blankets". PET is the most recyclable of the plastics.

LAYWOO-D3 is a composite of wood and polymer. It is similar to PLA, but after printing, it has the smell and appearance of wood. The surface can be rough or smooth on the same object.

Photopolymers are a class of liquid resins that cure or harden with a laser or light. Some create a solid that resembles ABS in its properties. Many are proprietary. Some are toxic, some are safe.

Stainless steel, bronze, tungsten, and copper are used in binder jetting and mixed with a binding agent, which is later removed and replaced with metal.

Tool steel, stainless steel, cobalt, chromium, nickel, titanium, and alloys of these are used in direct metal sintering and directed energy deposition printing to make solid metal objects.

3D printing and your health

Since 3D printing is a new technology, there may be problems that we don't know about. ABS sometimes gives off fumes when being printed because of the heat, but seems to be stable afterwards. Other materials like PLA can be food safe. But there are a lot of variables; the object could be dipped in acetone to smooth the surface, or there could be other additives mixed into the materials. The more common problem is that 3D printing processes may not create a completely smooth solid surface, so germs can find nice places to live. Currently, the only 3D-printed materials considered food safe are glazed ceramics and polished metals such as stainless steel. For printing food, chocolate, frosting, and so on, you need to make sure that the materials and the printer itself are food safe.

What happens at a 3D printing service?

It's a good idea to know at least a little about what happens between the time a 3D printing service receives your file and when you receive your object back. Here, Bart Veldhuizen, founder of BlenderNation, takes us on a tour of the Shapeways factory. It's very good for seeing all the steps involved in 3D printing:

- `http://vimeo.com/dezeen/print-shift-shapeways-3d-printing-tour`

Summary

You have learned a little about 3D printers and 3D printing. You discovered some opportunities for you to use your Blender design skills in 3D printing. We covered the fundamentals of how a 3D printer works and the different kinds of printers that there are. And you discovered that 3D printers can handle a wide variety of materials from wood, to plastic, to titanium. You learned a bit about factors to keep in mind when you are designing objects for 3D printing in Blender, such as the sizing and tolerances.

3D printing is an industry just taking off. It's time to join in the excitement and learn how to use Blender to make objects for 3D printing. Let's go!

2
Measuring and Texturing Techniques for 3D Printing

You have been given a general introduction to 3D printing. Now it's time to dive into preparing a file to be used in 3D printing. We will cover using the Ruler/Protractor to measure objects and texturing the model.

We'll be covering the following topics in this chapter:

- Precision modeling in Blender
- Using the Ruler/Protractor tool
- UV unwrapping
- Texture painting
- External textures

Precision modeling in Blender

With 3D printing, every object comes out of Blender into the real world. It must fit on the printing bed of a real 3D printer. It has real walls that must support the weight of the object; it's got real limits on how small or large the detail can be.

Nothing in the real world is perfect.

> One note on the instructions in this book. Sometimes several keys need to be pressed at the same time. These will be represented with a plus between them such as *Shift + D*. Press both keys at the same time.
>
> Pressing several keys in sequence will be represented by the word "press" followed by the keys separated by spaces, such as press *S Y 0 Enter*. You would press the *S* key, then the *Y* key, then the *0* key, and finally the *Enter* key.
>
> Some commands may use both, such as press *Shift + D Enter*. Here, you would press the *Shift* and the *D* key at the same time. Then you would press the *Enter* key.

1. Open **Blender** or open a new file by navigating to **File | New File** in the upper-left corner of the **Blender** window.

2. With the mouse over the **3D View**, press *Z* to get into wireframe mode.

3. Press *Shift + D Enter* to copy the default cube. Press *S* and use the mouse to scale up the cube. Do it quickly; don't worry about exact size. Select the original cube with the **RMB (Right Mouse Button)** and scale it quickly. Press *A* to deselect them.

4. Press *Shift + A* and navigate to **Mesh | UV Sphere**. Select **UV Sphere**. Press *Shift + D Enter*. Press *G* and move the sphere quickly in a direction. Select the other sphere and move it quickly in the same direction. Press *A*.

5. Press *Shift + A*. Navigate to **Mesh | Monkey**. Select **Monkey**. Press *Shift + D Enter*. Press *R* and rotate the monkey quickly. Select the other monkey and rotate it quickly. Press the *Home* key.

You notice that your cubes are not quite the same size. Your spheres did not end up in quite the same place and your monkeys did not rotate to quite the same angle. Unlike usual Blender 3D modeling where dimensions are precise, with 3D printing, there is always some variation in conditions that affect the 3D print. Different printers, different batches of plastic, different materials, and different temperatures all cause variations in the final print.

Allowing for these differences is called **tolerance**. It means that a measurement should be X but we'll accept it within a certain closeness of X. Some of the things that can create this tolerance were discussed in the *Factors affecting precision* section *Chapter 1, Designing Objects for 3D Printing*.

Look at the header at the bottom of the **3D View**. Note the 20 small boxes, arranged in groups of five. These boxes control the display of individual layers. The top 10 boxes control layers 1 to 10. The bottom 10 boxes control layers 11 to 20. Layer 11 is on the left and layer 20 is on the right. A dark grey box means that the level is visible. A light grey box means that the level is not visible. A grey dot indicates that there are objects in that level. An orange dot indicates that an active object is in that level. Pressing the *Shift* key while making a selection allows multiple levels to be selected.

For any questions about Blender's controls, the *Blender 3D Basics* book has an excellent introduction to the Blender user interface; check out *Chapter 2, Getting Comfortable Using the 3D View,* to learn how to set up and use basic controls such as the numpad, mouse, or keyboard on Mac, PC, and Linux. In this book, we will be giving instructions using the standard Blender controls.

Using the Ruler/Protractor

When building objects, you have to keep their dimensions and the ability of the 3D printer to reproduce them in mind. One of the handiest tools is a new tool called the Ruler/Protractor. It gives you a lot of power for measuring items, but can also be a bit tricky. Its operation may improve as it becomes more mature.

To learn how to use the Ruler/Protractor tool, let's use it to check how well a sword fits into its scabbard:

1. Load the file `45970S_02_Sword.blend` from the code bundle of this chapter. Press *Z* for wireframe display. Press the *Shift* button and select layer 11 to see the scabbard. At this point, the hilt is not important, so press *Shift* and select layer 2 to hide it.

2. Press *7* on the numpad to view the blade from the end. Look at the upper-left corner of the **3D View**. If you are not in Ortho mode, then press *5* on the numpad. Zoom in so you can see the scabbard and the blade clearly. It looks pretty good. The scabbard and the blade don't interfere with each other, and there is a little room all around the blade.

3. In the **Object Tools** subpanel of the **3D View** tool shelf, click on the **Ruler/ Protractor** button. Move to the left edge of the blade and press *Ctrl* + **LMB (Left Mouse Button)**. With the LMB pressed, move the cursor to the right edge of the blade. Then release the LMB. You will see a readout of the distance measured as seen in the following screenshot:

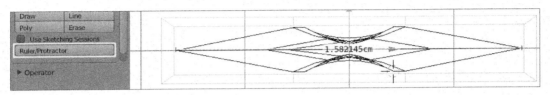

Don't worry if the readout that you see is not the same as in the screenshot. The **Ruler/Protractor** tool can be a little bit quirky, and we will discover how to get reliable measurements from it.

4. Press *1* on the numpad. Look at the left-hand end of the ruler. Zoom out so you can see to the end of the blade. Obviously, the ruler, as seen in the left-side of the following screenshot, isn't just measuring across the blade.

5. Select the left end of the ruler with the LMB and move it toward the top end of the blade. When you get it close, release the LMB and zoom in again. Pick up the end again with the LMB and move it close to the end of the blade. Press and hold the LMB and now press the *Ctrl* button and move the ruler end into place at the end of the blade. When you already have the LMB pressed, pressing the *Ctrl* button snaps the cursor to the nearest edge or vertex as seen on the right of the following screenshot.

6. Repeat this with the right end of the ruler if needed.

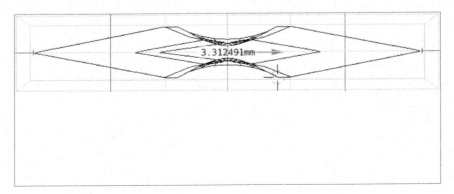

7. Press *7* on the numpad to see the end view again. Adjust the ends of the ruler if needed. I measured just over 3.3 mm as seen in the following screenshot:

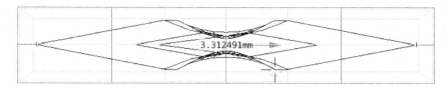

8. Now, move the cursor to the top of the blade. Press *Ctrl* + LMB and move down to the bottom of the blade. Move the cursor a little below the blade and notice how the cursor jumps between the blade and the scabbard. The *Ctrl* button snaps the end of the ruler to the nearest edge or vertex.

9. Press *1* on the numpad. Look at the new ruler carefully. Notice that the new ruler started at the same Z measurement that the first ruler was at. The last point has snapped to the corner of the blade. Rotate the view a little so you can see the first point separately from the first ruler. Select the first point and move it toward the end of the sword as seen on the right of the following screenshot. Press *7* on the numpad. Select the point again and start moving it. Then press *Ctrl* as you move it, and move it to the top of the blade. Then, after it snaps in place, press *7* and *1* on the numpad alternately to make sure it's in place. It's a little tricky, but now you can get an accurate measurement.

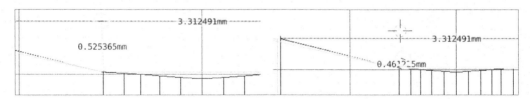

 Ctrl + *Z* to undo an operation does not work with the **Ruler/Protractor** tool. If you want to delete a ruler, press the *Delete* button.

The ruler is not associated with any specific object. You can snap its measurement between two different objects. Now that you have some idea of how the ruler works, try it for measuring the gap between the blade of the sword and the scabbard.

10. Now, check the vertical gap between the blade and the scabbard. Since you already have a measurement on the blade, start measuring from the scabbard.

You'll notice that the numerical readouts are not in mm or cm. These readings are in μm (micrometers or microns). I measured about 22 microns, or 0.022mm; that's tiny.

The specifications from one 3D printing service say that the accuracy for a detail-plastic copy of the sword would be ± 0.1 mm or 100 μm. Remember the last section, where you moved, rotated, and scaled the objects. The accuracy means that the measurement for the thickness of the sword could be 0.1 mm bigger than you intended, or it could be 0.1 mm smaller than you intended. The same holds true of the scabbard. You could get the sword turning out smaller and the scabbard turning out bigger; in this case, you'd have no problem. But if the sword turned out bigger and the scabbard turned out smaller, it wouldn't fit. This is called **stacking tolerances**, and must always be considered when making a multipart assembly. The following table lists possible outcomes of variations in the sword and scabbard:

		SWORD		
		Bigger	**Correct**	**Smaller**
SCABBARD	**Bigger**	???	Okay	Okay
	Correct	Bad	Okay	Okay
	Smaller	Bad	Bad	???

Do you think that the scabbard should be enlarged? Remember that the clearance between the sword and scabbard is about 1/5 of the minimum accuracy that the printing service might guarantee.

Using the Protractor

The **Ruler/Protractor** tool measures angles as well as lengths. Let's see how to do that:

1. Move the cursor to the middle of the ruler that you used to measure the distance from the top of the blade to the bottom of the blade.

2. Click the LMB and move the cursor toward the edge of the blade. The ruler becomes a protractor as seen in the following screenshot. It tells you the angle in degrees:

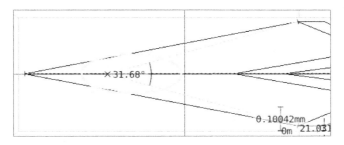

Measuring the thickness of an object

The **Ruler/Protractor** tool has one more trick. It will measure the thickness of an object:

1. Press the *Enter* key to get out of the Ruler/Protractor mode and save your rulers. Go to the **Visible Layers** display on the **3D View** header. Press *Shift* and click on layer 2 to display the hilt of the sword. Zoom out so you can see the hilt well.

2. In the **Object Tools** subpanel of the **3D View** tool shelf, click on the **Ruler/Protractor** button. Then choose an end of one of the rulers you have made. As you move it, press the *Shift* key and watch it automatically measuring the thickness of the object. Press the *Esc* key when you are done.

Remember that you can save these rulers and protractors or dispose of them. I have told you about deleting individual rulers. To get rid of all of them, just press *Esc* and the Ruler/Protractor mode will turn off and not save any of your tools. Press *Enter* and the rulers and protractors will be saved and Blender will exit Ruler/Protractor mode.

Preparing the model for coloring

The first difference to realize between making colors in Blender for 3D printing and the usual way of making colors in Blender is that you have less control. All you can control is the diffuse color. You cannot make the object shinier by adjusting the specularity, you cannot add transparency, or any of the other controls. In this respect, a 3D printer is like a regular printer. All it understands is a colored pixel. If you use transparency, at best it will show you the bare physical material underneath. Shininess, specularity, and so on are all properties of the material that you are printing with.

There are three ways to color your model:

- Leave the model uncolored and select a colored material when printing
- Assign colors to the polygons
- Assign a texture map to the polygons

Leaving the object uncolored

Many 3D printers do not handle color. This includes printers that print metal, extruded plastic, or liquid resins. The final color of the object comes from the material selected. Many colors and materials are available. You can dye or paint the objects after they are printed. The lunar lander in *Chapter 1, Designing Objects for 3D Printing*, was printed in this way. It was printed in white nylon then dyed yellow and grey. Next, the joystick was painted red and black with acrylic paint and a small image of the lander's touchscreen from a standard color copier was glued into place. Blender exports an STL file for printers like these.

Vertex colors

Assigning color to the polygons is the easiest way, but it's also the most limited because your minimum detail is constrained by the size of the polygon. When you select a polygon and assign a color to it, the color is assigned to all vertices of the polygon:

1. Open **Blender** or press *Ctrl + N* for a new file. With the default cube selected, press the *Tab* key to go into edit mode.

2. In the Properties panel header on the right, select the shiny ball. This opens the Materials panel.

3. In the Diffuse subpanel, set the color to red.

4. Click on **Assign**. The first material assigned to an object is assigned to all polygons by default.

5. Click on the plus sign to the right of your red material. Click on the **New** button. Set the Diffuse color to `yellow`.

6. Press *A* to deselect all of the vertices. Press *C* and then move the mouse over four vertices in a polygon while pressing the LMB. Press the RMB when you are done and click on the **Assign** button.

7. Press *F12* to render the scene and view it. Then return to the **3D View** window by pressing *Esc*.

That's pretty simple, and when it is printed, you will have a red cube with one yellow side.

Vertex painting

Blender has painting tools included to do vertex painting, which is much easier than just selecting faces and assigning them colors and produces a better result. Vertex painting allows you to set the colors vertex-by-vertex. Then, the computer blends the color between the vertices. So, between a blue vertex and a white vertex, the edge and part of the face will go from blue to light blue to white. Let's see how vertex painting works:

1. Press *Tab* to go from **Edit Mode** to **Object Mode**. Press *A* to deselect the cube. Press *Shift + A* and navigate to **Mesh | UVSphere** from the menu. Select **UV Sphere**. Press *G* and use the mouse to move the sphere to the right of the cube. Press the LMB to stop moving the sphere. Zoom in so you can see the sphere better.

2. Press *V* to go into vertex paint mode. The sphere turns white, and in the toolbox on the left of the **3D View**, there is a color palette and paint brush controls. Choose a color and set the radius of the paint brush to `15`. Put the cursor over the sphere. Press the LMB and move the mouse to paint some of the sphere.

3. Change the color and paint more of the sphere. Choose a third color and just press the LMB to do small dabs of paint. Notice how it only paints at the vertices, not everywhere.

4. Go to the **Properties** panel. Make a new material. Scroll down to the **Options** subpanel and check **Vertex Color Paint**. Press *F12* to render.

Pretty easy! You can see how the colors are centered at the vertices and blended between them. Feel free to play a little more with coloring and rendering.

Building texture maps

The most powerful way of adding a texture to your object is by using a texture map. Do not use a texture map and vertex colors on the same object, especially if the two methods share a vertex. The 3D printer may not choose the right material.

> Make sure you delete any unwanted materials before exporting your object for 3D printing. This is easy. With your object selected, just select the materials button on the **Properties** window header. It's the one that looks like a chrome ball. At the top will be a list of the materials assigned to the active object. If you click on them, the **Preview** window will display a preview of that material. To delete the material, simply click on the minus button to the right of the list of materials.

Texture mapping gives you the best control over the color of any part of the surface. It also gives you controls so you can assign the locations of different regions of the texture and use another program such as Gimp or Photoshop to create fine details.

Choosing colors for printing

The most common colored 3D printing material is gypsum, sometimes called sandstone. The following graphic is a chart of colors used in printing full color sandstone:

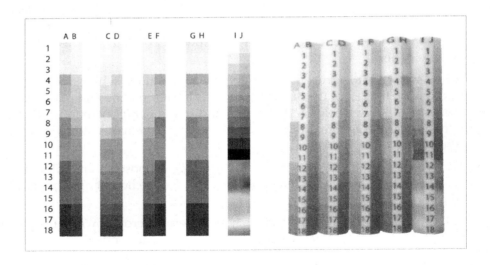

You get them from the printing service. The chart on the left-hand side of the preceding diagram shows you a range of colors. The bars on the right-hand side are 3D-printed samples printed with the same colors. Look at the printed samples to choose the printed color you want. Read the index number off of the samples. Then, use a program such as Gimp or Photoshop to get the exact RGB values of the indexed color which you can use to specify the exact color in Blender.

This is a useful tool because the colors printed are not always exactly as you specify them. You can see this if you look at one color in the previous chart and samples. And indeed, the printing service specifies that no two samples may be exactly the same. So it's a rough guide, not an exact one. A copy of the chart on the left-hand side is in your download kit as 4597OS_02_01.png.

UV unwrapping

UV mapping is a way of assigning a section of a graphic image to the face of a polygon. This is done by a process called unwrapping the UV mapping. The letters U and V describe the horizontal and vertical axes of a bitmap image. The letters U and V are used to avoid confusion with the X, Y, and Z geometry coordinates.

Creating UV maps may seem intimidating, but it's not that difficult. To unwrap the UV mapping, you select a polygon and press the **UV Unwrap** button. Then, Blender assigns a pair of UV coordinates to each vertex of the polygon and gives them an initial value. Next, in the **UV/Image editor** window, an image is displayed with an overlay that shows where the UV coordinates for the polygon are with respect to the image. You then move these coordinates around until they are over the section of the image that you want to be displayed on the face of that polygon.

Next, you will do some texture mapping onto a model of a dragon that we will be working on for most of the rest of the book. We will decorate its wings, its chest, and its head.

UV mapping the wings

We will start by applying UV maps to the wings. This will give us good practice in moving the UV coordinates as groups:

1. Open 4597OS_02_Dragon_Untextured.blend from the code bundle.

2. In the **Properties** panel, turn the visibility controls for the **Mirror** and **Subsurf** modifiers off; they look like eyes. Half of the dragon will disappear and it will look very blocky. The **Mirror** and **Subsurf** modifiers will be used in *Chapter 3, Making a Blender Model that's Ready to Print*, and *Chapter 4, Making Strong, Light Objects with the Solidify Modifier*, but they are not needed now.

3. Press *Tab* to get into **Edit Mode**. Press 3 on the numpad to get a side view. Click on the **Face Select** button.

4. The lower-left window is the **UV/Image Editor**. Select **Image** from the header and then choose **New Image** from the popup menu.

5. For the dragon's general color, I chose the color square D12 from the chart in the preceding image. Its value is 0.224 Red, 0.58 Green, and 0 Blue. Use those values for the background color of the image. The size should be 1024 x 1024. Then, click on **OK**. Press **Home** to see the entire image.

6. In the **3D View**, pan down and zoom in so you can see all of the leading edge of the wing as shown in the next screenshot. Press C and select the faces of the front of the wing as seen in the next screenshot. Do not select the faces of the very edge of the wing, just these 5 faces on the side of the wing. Press the RMB to stop selecting.

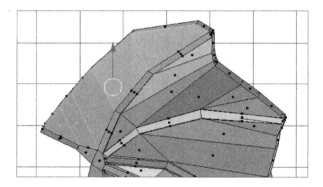

7. This is the membrane of the wing. The narrow sections on either side of the membrane are the dragon's fingers. Select the rest of the membrane areas, as seen in the following screenshot:

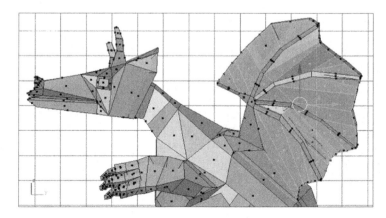

8. Select **Mesh** from the **3D View** header. Then, navigate to **UV Unwrap | Unwrap** from the pop-up menus. Select **Unwrap**. In the **UV/Image Editor**, your green image disappears and is replaced by the UV coordinates of the polygons that you have just unwrapped, as seen in the following screenshot:

9. To get your image back, select the **Browse Image to be linked** button which is to the left-hand side of the **New** button, as seen in the previous screenshot, and select your green **Untitled** image from the pop-up menu. Press *Home* to see the whole image.

10. In the Properties panel, select the **Object Data** button that looks like a triangle. In the **Vertex Groups** subpanel, click on the plus button and create a new vertex group. Name it `Texture - Outer Wing`. Assign the faces to it. This assigns all the faces that are currently selected in the **3D View** to the vertex group.

Using **Vertex Groups** to organize your sections of texture is very important. It means you will never have to go through selecting the faces again. This gives you a lot of flexibility if you make a mistake and greater control when working with the UV maps.

The first thing that you notice when you look at the **UV/Image Editor** is that the mapping of the UV coordinates does not resemble the shape of the wing. You want to reorganize the UV coordinates so that they do:

1. Find the section that resembles the first membrane that you selected. Select one UV coordinate on it with the RMB. Press *L* and the whole membrane section is selected, as seen on the left-hand side of the following screenshot:

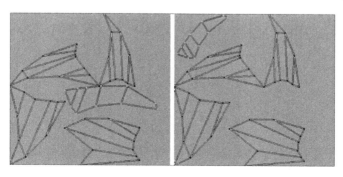

2. Now, rotate this group of UV coordinates into the same orientation that the faces are in the **3D View** window. Press *R* and rotate the coordinates so they are at the same angle as in the **3D View**. Press *S* and scale them so they cover a little less than a quarter of the height of the green image. Press *G* to move them to the top-left corner of the image as seen in the right-hand side of the preceding screenshot.

3. Select the next section of membrane in the same way as you selected the first. It's the upper-left one that you have not modified, as seen on the left-hand side of the following screenshot:

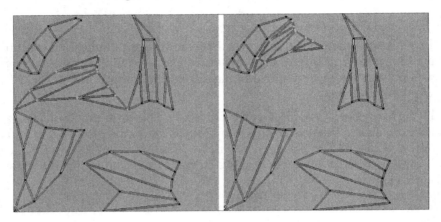

4. Rotate, scale, and move it so it is snug with the first membrane section as seen on the right-hand side of the preceding screenshot. Leave a gap between them where the fingers of the wing should be.

5. Next, repeat this with the third membrane. It's the one in the lower-left corner. There is a trick with this one. If you look carefully, you'll see it's backwards in X. So, first press *S X -1 Enter*. This will flip the UV coordinates along the x axis. Then rotate, scale, and move it into place next to the other two membranes.

6. Now move, rotate, and scale the fourth membrane into place.

7. Repeat this with the membrane between a finger and the dragon's body. Now it looks like a wing, as seen on the left-hand side of the following screenshot:

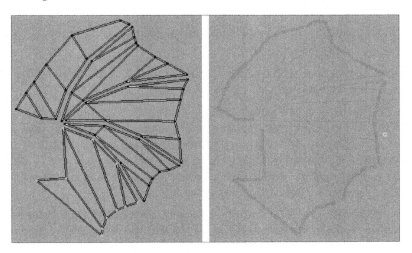

Good. Since the UV coordinates are now laid over the image in a shape like the faces of the wing, when you paint the wing, you will know which part of your image is mapped to which part of the wing. Now, to help us remember which section of the image has already been used, let's outline it:

1. There are two buttons labeled **View** in the **UV/Image Editor** header. Choose the one in the center of the header with the icon of an image. Select **Paint** from the pop-up menu.

2. Press *N* to get the **UV/Image Editor** properties panel. Scroll down to the Paint subpanel. Set the color to red. Set the radius of the brush to 5.

3. Use the *Ctrl* + **MMB (Middle Mouse Button)** to zoom into the part of the image where you see the UV faces and *Shift* + MMB to pan. Outline the faces as done in the preceding screenshot. You are just marking the area where the UV coordinates of the outer wing are so you will know what areas of the image are still available to put the other UV coordinates that you create.

4. Click on the button labeled **Paint** and choose **View** from the pop-up menu.

Congratulations, you have texture mapped the outer side of the wing. Now it's time to do the inner side:

1. Move the cursor over the **3D View** window. Press *Ctrl + 3* on the numpad to see the other side of the dragon. In the **Vertex Groups** subpanel of the **Properties** panel, click on the plus button and create a vertex group named `Texture - Inner Wing`.

2. Press *A* to deselect all the faces. Press *C* and select the faces of the inner side of the wing membrane.

3. Assign these vertices to the `Texture - Inner Wing` group. Now, UV unwrap the inner side of the wing membranes just as you did for the outer side. Use the `UV Unwrap` command, display your Untitled image, and move the UV coordinates. Be sure to start building your mapping from the upper-right corner of the image at about the same size as the outer wing was mapped. Do each section as before.

4. If you get stuck and you can't figure out which of the membranes is which, make sure you have assigned the vertices to the `Texture - Inner Wing` group. Then, in the **3D View**, press *A* to deselect all faces and then select a face from the membrane whose UV coordinates you want to move. They will appear in the **UV/Image Editor** and you can note where they are. Then, go to the **Vertex Groups** subpanel and click on **Select** to have all the faces of the inner wing appear.

5. Once all of the membranes are in place relative to each other, press *A* in the **UV/Image Editor** to select all of them then scale the whole so it is about as large as the outer wing as seen in the following screenshot:

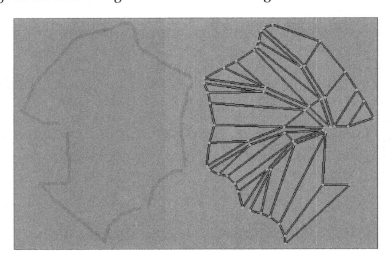

6. Paint an outline around the inner wing to mark where it is.

7. Save your Blender file. Then, go down to the **UV/Image editor** header. There is an * next to the word Image. This means that the image in the **UV/Image editor** has been changed since it was last saved. Click on **Image** then choose **Save As Image** from the pop-up menu. Save it in the same folder as your Blender file. You never know what kind of folder structure the printer is using, so it's best to keep them together.

UV mapping the belly

Now we map the dragon's belly. This will give us practice in modifying individual UV coordinates.

Now, it's time to texture the dragon's belly:

1. Press *A* to deselect all the polygons. Press *C* and select the column of polygons from the dragons, chin down to his bottom as seen in the following screenshot. Don't select the polygons on his tail.

2. Make a new vertex group named `Texture - Belly` and assign the vertices to it.

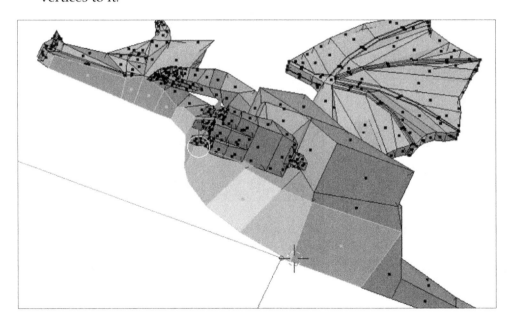

3. Unwrap the UVs and display your image again.

4. Move the cursor over the top row of edges in the **UV/Image Editor**. Press *Alt + RMB* to select the top row of edges. Press *S Y 0 Enter*. This will put all of the selected UV coordinates at the same height.

5. Repeat these steps for the bottom edges. The edges will now be parallel.

6. Now, move the UV coordinates of the bottom row one-by-one so that the vertical edges are straight up and down. After selecting a UV coordinate, pressing *G X* before you move it will limit your motion to the X direction and make control much easier.

7. Select all of the UV coordinates. Move them almost to the bottom as seen in the following screenshot. Leave a little room below them though.

8. Go into **Paint** mode and outline where the top row of UV coordinates are. Return to **View** mode from **Paint** mode.

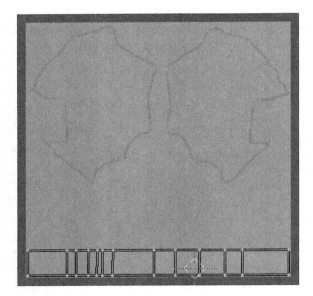

9. The reason for making the top and bottom rows parallel is that now if you make scales all of the same size in your art, they will appear smaller when they are at the neck than at the bottom of the dragon's belly.

UV mapping the edges of the wing

Mapping the edges of the wings is very similar to mapping the belly and the wings. First you work with groups of UV coordinates, then you work with individual UV coordinates:

1. In the **3D View** window, press *A* to deselect all polygons. Rotate your view so you can see the edge of the dragon's wing. Select the edge of the membranes as seen in the following screenshot. Do not select the edge of the fingers:

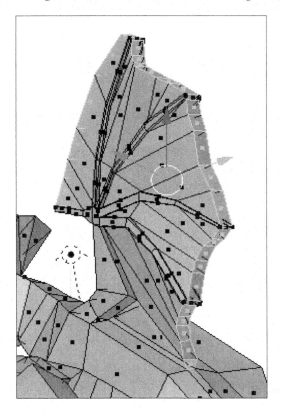

2. In the Properties panel, make a `Texture - Edge Wing` vertex group. Assign the faces to it.

3. UV unwrap them. What a mess. What we want to do is line all of the UV coordinates into two nice rows. Remember about deselecting all of them and choosing some faces in the **3D View** as a way to get your bearings? Start at the front of the wing and work your way to the back.

4. Move the faces of the edge so that they are in an approximate line. With the mouse over the **UV/Image editor**, press A to deselect all the UV coordinates. Press *Shift + Alt* + RMB to select the entire top row section-by-section as seen in the following screenshot:

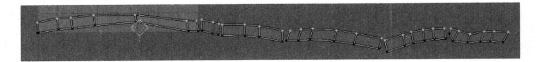

5. Press *S Y 0 Enter*. Then, press *G Y* and move the top row up a little so that the two rows do not overlap.

6. Select the bottom row only. Press *S Y 0 Enter*. Press *G Y* and move that row up so it is about as thick as the UV coordinates were originally.

7. Select all of the UV coordinates. Get your image background displayed in the **UV/Image Editor**.

8. Scale the UV coordinates so that they fit in the image area. Move them just above the area for the belly, as seen in the following screenshot. Paint a red line on the graphic at the top of the area they occupy to mark where they are.

Note the solitary orange dot near the lower-left corner of the following screenshot. This is a quirk of Blender. You selected only the faces of the edge of the membranes. But, since the faces on the end of the fingers shared vertices with the edges of the membranes, Blender also picked them up. Since you did not choose them, it did not assign them any area on the UV map. It just lumped them all together in one spot. This will work; just make sure that they are all mapped to an area with the background green. Use the C or B command to select them if you want to move them.

UV mapping the head

With the UV coordinates of the head, we will learn to adjust the UV coordinates to emphasize certain details, giving us more of the texture map to use on these details and allowing us more creative control:

1. Save your image file and your Blender file.

2. With the cursor over the **3D View** window, press *A* to deselect all faces. Now, select the polygons of the dragon's head. Do not select the area under the chin because you have already assigned that to the belly. Do not choose any polygons on the back of the frill or the neck. Rotate your view to be sure you get the nose, the corner of the mouth, and all sides of the horns.

3. Make a vertex group, `Texture - Head`, and assign the vertices to it. UV unwrap it and display the green texture map image.

4. Select all the UV coordinates in the **UV/Image Editor**. If the nose is at the bottom, you will need to scale the dragon's head; if you do, press *S Y -1 Enter* to get it into the proper orientation. Now, scale, rotate, and move the UV coordinates so that they fill the remaining available area in the texture map as seen in the following screenshot. Draw an outline around it:

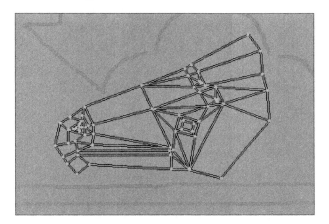

5. Save your files. You now have your dragon texture mapped.

6. You may want to take some time to make adjustments to the mapping. Have the UV coordinate sets cover as much of the image area as possible. The greater the area that these sets cover, the more pixels are mapped to them. The more pixels that are mapped to a face, the more detailed the texture can be.

You may have noticed that we have not texture mapped the entire dragon. In the following chapters, we will modifying some of the geometry to put a pen cup into his back. This will destroy the UV mapping of any faces that are involved. Only the faces on the center of the dragon's back are affected, not the wings. But Blender does provide a default UV mapping in this case. It takes the four corner pixels of the texture map and uses the average of these four pixels as the color for all unmapped polygons. So, make sure that none of your UV coordinate faces cover the four corner pixels of the image.

Painting the texture map

It's time to paint your texture. You have a choice of methods. You can continue to use the **Paint** tool in the **UV/Image Editor**, or you can export your UV maps as a .png file for use in another program such as Gimp, Photoshop, or whatever you prefer.

Exporting the UV Layout for use in an external paint program

Exporting the UV Layout lets you have the power of the best graphics programs for making a texture map. When you export the UV Layout, it is in the form of a .png file that you can read into another graphics program. One layer will be an image of all of the UV coordinate locations. Make an image on other layers, using the coordinate layer to guide you. Turn the coordinate's layer off when you are done and save a bitmap copy of the finished graphic. Then, bring it back into Blender as a texture map for the object.

It's easy to export your UV map. Display all of the UV coordinates that you want to show up on the map and use the Export UV Layout function:

1. To export your UV map, change from **Paint** to **View**.

2. In the **Vertex Group** subpanel of the **Properties** panel, for each of the vertex groups, choose the UV map and then click on the **Select** button.

3. Select **UVs** from the **UV/Image Editor** header. Choose **Export UV Layout** from the pop-up menu. Put this map into the same directory as your Blender file. Choose a name and then press the **Export UV Layout** button in the top-right of the page. This will create a .png file with a layer that you can use as a guide to creating a texture map for your dragon.

Painting your texture in Blender

You can also create a texture map using Blender's paint tools. This may be more convenient, even though you don't have quite as much control as you get in a dedicated graphics program such as Gimp or Photoshop.

Now you can paint the image in the UV/Image editor. You'll then save your file and create a material that employs the UV mapping work that you've done and mates it up to the texture map that you make:

1. To use the **Paint** tool, return to **Paint** mode. Paint the wings of your dragon. Paint the outer wing, the inner wing, and the wing edge.

2. Return to **View** mode. Save your image file to a new name. It's time to apply the texture.

3. In the Properties panel, select the Materials button in the header; it's the one with the chrome ball on it. Click on the **New** button to make a new material.

4. Now, click on the checkerboard button next to the Materials button. Click on the **New** button. Click on the **Type:** button where it says **Clouds**. Select **Image or Movie** from the pop-up menu.

5. Scroll down to the **Image** subpanel. Select **Open**. Choose the .png file you just saved.

6. Scroll down to the **Mapping** subpanel. Click on the **Coordinates:** button where it says **Generated**. Choose **UV** from the pop-up menu.

7. Press *F12*. You will render the dragon with its wings painted. Save the file. Press *Esc* to close the rendered image.

Modifying the UV coordinates to add detail

You can also modify the UV coordinates to use more of the texture map for more important details and use less of the texture map on less important details. Here, you add more detail to the horn on his head by adjusting the UV coordinates and painting on the texture map:

1. In the **UV/Image Editor**, zoom into the inner horn as seen on the left-hand side of the following screenshot. It's kind of small. Get into **View** mode. Move the UV coordinates out to cover more of the texture map and organize them as seen in the center of the following screenshot.

2. Next, go into **Paint** mode and paint it as seen on the right. You don't have to copy what I did though. Then, return to **View** mode and save the image to the same name as you did before.

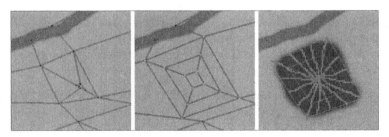

3. In the **Image** subpanel of the texture panel in the properties window, click on the button with the opposing arrows to reload the texture file. Press *F12* to render the dragon.

Using the Clone brush to add detail

Now, as a final touch, we will explore how to add better detail to the texture map by bringing in an outside graphic and duplicating the patterns from it.

1. In the **UV/Image Editor**, pan down to the area reserved for the dragon's belly. Go into **Paint** mode. In the **Paint** subpanel of the **UV/Image Editor** properties panel, choose the **F Clone** brush. The brush selection is just below where it says **Paint**. Set the radius of the brush to about 25 and the strength to 1.0.

2. In the **UV/Image Editor** header, select **Image**. Select **Open Image** from the pop-up menu. Choose 45970S_02_02.png in the Images directory. Press *Home*.

3. Select your texture map with your wings from the header again.

4. In the **Paint** subpanel on the left-hand side of the **UV Image** properties panel, click on the picture button next to **Image:**. Select 45970S_02_02.png. The image of the scales will appear at the bottom of the UV/Image Editor window.

5. In the **UV/Image editor**, zoom in to the area of the belly. Use the Clone brush over the belly area.

6. When you have finished painting the clone area, return to View and save the image. In the Image subpanel of the Properties panel, refresh the texture as you did after painting the horn. Press F12 to render the dragon.

Now, something may look odd. The dragon's body is a different shade of green than its head is as seen in the following screenshot. Remember about the pixels in the corner that I mentioned in the last information box? You probably painted over two of the corner pixels when you used the Clone brush. But that is easy to fix:

1. Return to **Paint** mode. Choose the **F Brush**. Click on the brush color button below the color wheel. Another color wheel pops up. Click on the eyedropper button on the popup color wheel. And click the eyedropper cursor over a green part of the image. Set the radius of the brush to 2 and the strength to 1.0.

2. Paint the bottom-left corner and right-corner pixels of the image green. Don't paint into the UV area of the belly. If UV coordinates extend to the corner, select them and move them up a few pixels. Retouch the scales with the F Clone brush if needed.

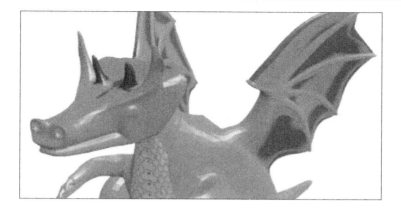

3. Return to **View** mode. Save the image and the Blender file. Then refresh the texture as you did after painting the horn. Rerender it and it should be fine.

4. Now you can paint the eye, and if you want, paint a little blood on its lips.

Summary

Now you have a good idea of how to use the Ruler/Protractor tool and how to unwrap a UV map, paint a texture map, and apply it to the object. You also learned how to use the F Clone brush to create a texture that is more detailed than you would want to do with the Blender painting system.

In the next chapter you will be introduced to what it takes to properly make a Blender model for 3D printing. You will learn how to measure it precisely and how to make the object so it will come out correctly into the real world.

3

Making a Blender Model that's Ready to Print

You learned how to use the **Ruler/Protractor** tool so that you can do precision modeling, and reviewed how to create colored and textured objects. Now it's time to get to the core of this book and make a printer-ready 3D model in Blender. This chapter teaches you how to make models that are **watertight**, **manifold**, and will print well.

The following are the topics we'll be covering in this chapter:

- Using the 3D Print Toolbox panel and the Mesh Analysis panel
- Selecting the units to use
- Making a model watertight
- Making a model manifold
- Dealing with distorted faces and sharp edges
- Economizing-getting the most object for the least cost

What is special about 3D printing?

Blender has always been able to make models suitable for 3D printing. But starting with Blender 2.67, they included two new tools that make it much easier, the **Mesh Analysis** panel and the **3D Print Toolbox** panel. We'll look at both of them and then use them to make sure our model is fit for 3D printing.

Installing the Print3D toolbox

The **Print 3D Toolbox** panel is an add-on to Blender. The first thing you need to do is install it and perform the following steps:

1. Open up Blender or select **File | New | Reload Start-up File**, or press *Ctrl + N*.

2. Open up the User Preferences panel, either by selecting **File | User Preferences...** or by pressing *Ctrl + Alt + U*.

3. In the pop-up window, select **Addons** from the menu at the top.

4. When the **Addons** menu page appears, there are two sets of menus, as seen in the following screenshot, one on the left and one on the right. Select the **Mesh** button at the lower-left corner:

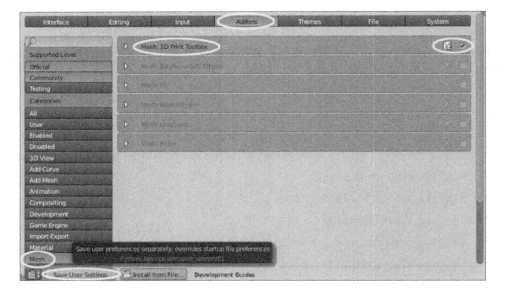

5. Find the selection labeled **Mesh: 3D Print Toolbox** in the right-hand menu. Check the checkbox. At the lower-left corner of the window, select the **Save User Settings** button so that the 3D Print Toolbox will automatically be included with Blender on startup.

6. Then click on the large red **X** at the upper-right corner of the window to close the **Blender User Preferences** window.

7. Now the **Print3D** toolbox will be available to you in the **Tool Shelf** on the left-hand side of the 3D View window.

Introducing the Print3D toolbox

The **Print3D** toolbox is located in **Tool Shelf** on the right-hand side of the 3D View window. It has 3 main sections, as seen in the following screenshot. The first, on the left, has buttons for the checks you can perform and statistics you can get about the object. The second, seen in the center, has tools for cleanup and exporting the model. The third, shown on the right, gives you a readout of what has been found and buttons to display the affected polygons.

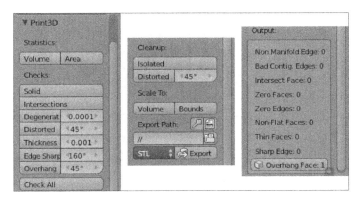

Introducing the Mesh Analysis panel

The Mesh Analysis panel performs similar functions to the Print3D Toolbox, but it has a more graphic interface and is more interactive. It's located in the 3D View Properties panel on the right-hand side of the 3D View window. You must be in edit mode to see it:

1. Open the `4597_03_Distorted Cube.blend` file. This distorted cube is a very bad candidate for 3D printing. Make sure you are in **Edit Mode** and scroll down in the Properties panel of the 3D View window until you see the **Mesh Analysis** subpanel.

2. Click on the **Mesh Analysis** checkbox. The **Type:** button says **Sharp**. The distorted cube has become colored. Polygons that are not too sharp are displayed in grey. The sharper the geometry, the more the color goes from blue to red as seen in the following screenshot:

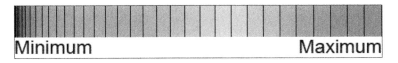

3. Rotate the cube around; look at the bottom as well as the point. The two buttons below the **Type:** button mark the minimum and maximum angles you are inspecting for. Play with their values. They let you choose a range of values that you want to watch for.

4. Click on the **Type:** button and select **Distortion**. Rotate the cube and notice the coloration. The two buttons below mark the minimum and maximum angles you are inspecting for. Play with their values. Can you see any distorted polygons?

5. Click on the **Type:** button and select **Intersect**. There are no degrees to intersection; polygons either intersect or they don't.

6. Next is **Thickness**. It measures the thickness of the object. You can choose a range with the min and max buttons. For a more graphic display, select all the vertices, press *W*, and subdivide the faces of the cube to about four or five cuts. Then inspect it again.

7. The last category is **Overhang**, which is a problem for material extrusion printers like most hobbyist printers. You'll notice that initially, the top surface of the cube is overhanging and red. Play with the min, max buttons and select the different **X**, **Y**, and **Z** buttons. They define overhang according to different axes.

The **Mesh Analysis** panel gives you powerful tools to use in determining what needs to be fixed on your model to make it printable. You can adjust the minimum and maximum values to trap a range of values which will tell you a lot about the geometry.

Setting up the units of the scene

Metric units are the default standard of measurement in 3D printing. To set up Blender for **Metric** scaling, navigate to the Blender Properties panel and select the button with the **lamp**, **sphere**, and **cylinder** icon from the header as seen in the following screenshot. Then, scroll down until you see the **Units** subpanel. Select the **Metric** button, and then set the **Scale** option to **0.001** (thousandths of a meter, or a millimeter). Millimeters will be the scale we are using.

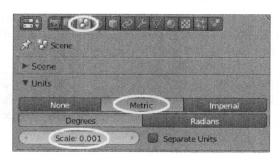

There is a reason for this. If you make something very tiny, like a detailed HO scale train body and you use meters as your unit, you will be more likely to run into rounding errors where the numbers you are using are too small for the computer. They will get mangled and so will your model. Of course, if you are modeling something bigger, like a full-sized copy of an Aston Martin DB4, you may want to work in meters.

There are several ways to see Ivan Sentch's ambitious Aston Martin 3D printing project. The builder has the following website and a Facebook page. The website also goes into a lot of issues that people making models for 3D printers face:

- `http://www.replicadb4.com/`
- `https://www.facebook.com/ReplicaDB4`

Designboom has a nice overview of the project with many good pictures (`http://www.designboom.com/design/3d-printed-aston-martin-db4-replica-by-ivan-sentch/`).

Making a 3D model that will print

Modeling for 3D printing is the same as any other modeling in Blender. But there are no cheats. You have to be precise and orderly. Using the **Mesh Analysis** panel hinted at the kinds of things we are looking to eliminate, such as intersecting polygons, holes in the model, sharp edges, polygons that aren't flat, and details that are too small or too delicate. We are making objects for the real world and must always consider that. We have to remember what material we are going to make the part with, how large it is, and how precisely we have to fit it together with other objects.

3D printing is an art, not a science. Many times, the only thing to do is to try something and see if it works. A file that works with one printer or material may fail with another. But there are considerations that are universal. The two big words for 3D printing are watertight and manifold.

Making a watertight model

With 3D printing, we are trying to bring our Blender objects into the real world. Real objects are solid. They have height, width, and depth. So, an object modeled in Blender for 3D printing has to be solid as well. There can't be any gaps between polygons. The polygons of an object must enclose a volume of space completely. When they do, the object is called watertight.

Consider a beach ball, as seen on the left of the following screenshot. It surrounds a volume of air completely. There are no gaps in the surface. If you throw it in the water, it will float because the water cannot get inside. It's watertight.

If you cut the top off the beach ball, as in the center of the screenshot, then throw it in the water, it does not completely surround a volume of air. There's a big gap in the surface. Water can get in and it will sink. It's not watertight.

But, if you give the beach ball a second inner wall, as seen on the right, and then make sure that the inner wall and outer wall are sealed to each other, then they completely surround a volume of air between the walls. No water can get inside these walls, so it will float. It is watertight:

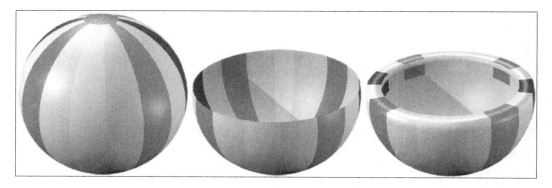

You should also remember that you cannot control how well people will be able to see your model. They can get up close with a magnifying glass if they like. You can't cut corners the way you might if you are only rendering an object. So, you want to make your model tight and pretty anyway.

Making a manifold model

Manifold is a more mysterious term. The word doesn't come up in regular conversation.

There are two conditions for being manifold:

- A manifold vertex is the one that is connected to another vertex by an edge
- A manifold edge is the one that has exactly two polygons associated with it

This may seem rather restrictive at first, but it's not. Non-manifold edges are edges that have any other number of polygons associated with them. This would include edges with zero polygons, one polygon, three polygons, four, five, six, and more. They would be very confusing to a printer.

Think about it. How could a printer print an edge without a polygon? There is nothing to print. An edge that is associated only with one polygon can't be printed either. A single polygon does not surround any volume. When you have an edge with three or more polygons, the outermost polygons will define a volume and any other edges will be within the volume, as shown in the following screenshot. On the right-hand side of the screenshot is a manifold edge attached to two polygons. There are no conflicts and the polygons can contain a volume:

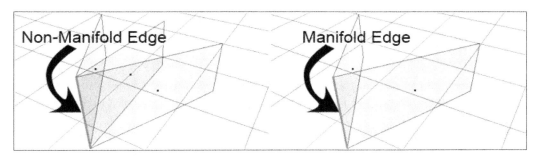

 It should be noted that the two examples in the preceding screenshot are meant to demonstrate only whether a single edge is manifold or non manifold.

Inspecting objects to see if they are manifold or non-manifold

This next exercise will give you some practice in identifying manifold edges. You will get a number of objects to inspect. See what you think:

1. Go back to Blender and open the `4597_03_Distorted Cube.blend` file again. Press *Z* to set the display mode to wireframe. Look at it closely. Can you find the edge that is shared by three polygons? Can you find the two edges associated with only a single polygon? The distorted cube is not manifold.

2. Press *Tab* to get into object mode. Press *X* to delete the distorted cube.

3. Press *Shift + A*. Select **Mesh | UV Sphere**. Press *Tab* to get into edit mode. Look at it closely. Observe that all edges share exactly two polygons, no more, no less, even at the top and bottom. It is a nice solid object, manifold, and can be 3D printed.

4. Look at the **Mesh** objects, **Cube**, **Torus**, and **Cone**; they are manifold as well.

Finding problems that make a file non-manifold

Now that you've had a quick example of manifold and non-manifold edges, it's time to use the **Print3D Toolbox** panel to find non-manifold edges. You may use the file of the dragon that you made in *Chapter 2, Measuring and Texturing Techniques for 3D Printing*, or you can use 4597_03_Dragon.blend from your download directory and perform the following steps:

1. Load the file and make sure you are in Object mode.

2. Scroll down in the 3D View toolbox to the **Print3D** subpanel. Click on the **Solid** button.

3. In the **Output** section of the subpanel, it says that there are 56 non-manifold edges. Get in to Edit mode. Click on the **Non Manifold Edges** button in the **Output** section of the **Print3D** subpanel to display the problem areas.

4. Press *Z* to set the 3D View shading to **Wireframe**. You may want to temporarily turn off the **Mirror** and **Subsurface** modifiers to make it easier to see the non-manifold edges. The controls are in the Properties panel on the right. Click on the wrench symbol in the header to get the modifiers panel. Then, toggle the eye symbols for the **Mirror** and **Subsurface** modifiers so they are a light grey.

5. Most of the non-manifold edges are because of the **Mirror** modifier and lie on the YZ axis plane. There are 39 of them. Don't worry about them. They will resolve themselves when you apply the **Mirror** modifier in the next chapter. But there are seven other problems with the dragon. The problem edges are displayed in orange.

These problems are typical of small errors that can happen in models. They won't bother you if you animate in Blender, but will affect the 3D printer. They are as follows:

- A non-manifold vertex without an edge (this will not show up on the count of non-manifold edges but might cause problems printing)

- A non-manifold edge without any polygon

- A non-manifold edge from a polygon to a single vertex

- A non-manifold edge between vertices of two different polygons, but not associated with any polygon

- Four non-manifold edges surrounding a polygon (the polygon may be unneeded)

- Two vertices that are very, very close together and have separate edges when they should be in the same location and share edges, so they leave a tiny hole in the surface

- A missing polygon causing a hole in the surface

Now you will begin to prepare the dragon for printing by eliminating the non-manifold parts of the model. Compare the list to the problem areas highlighted when you click on the **Non Manifold Edges:** button and one by one eliminate the problems:

1. Open up a **Text Editor** window below the Blender Properties panel, click on the button with the image of the spiral notebook to find a text named **Non Manifold Text**. It has a list of the items you are to find. You can use this to keep track of which problems you have found.

2. Find them and fix them. Every time you find one of the errors and fix it, press the **Solid** button in the **Print3D** subpanel again to refresh the list of non-manifold edges. Then, click on the **Non Manifold Edges:** button to display what is still to be found. You'll see the count go down to **39** as you remove problems. It is easiest if you work on problems with edges first.

3. You can also use the command *Ctrl + Alt + Shift + M* to display non-manifold edges.

 To examine a vertex, edge, or face more closely, use the . key on the numpad after you select a vertex, edge. The selected vertex, edge, or face will then be the center of rotation for your view.

If you have searched and have not found the non-manifold vertex without an edge, click on the **Isolated** button in the **Cleanup** section of the **Print3D** subpanel. It removes any isolated edges and vertices. In the **Output:** section, it will tell you **Verts Removed: 1**.

Fixing noncontiguous edges

Below the **Non Manifold Edge:** button, there is a button labeled **Bad Contig. Edges:**. This is short for bad contiguous edges. It identifies polygons that share an edge but do not make a smooth surface. The following screenshot shows what this looks like. Most of the normals on this surface are facing up as shown by the thin blue lines. A few of the polygons have normals facing down. Their blue lines point away and are hidden by the solid polygons.

The **Bad Contig. Edges:** function identifies adjoining polygons which have normals facing in different directions by drawing the edge between them in orange.

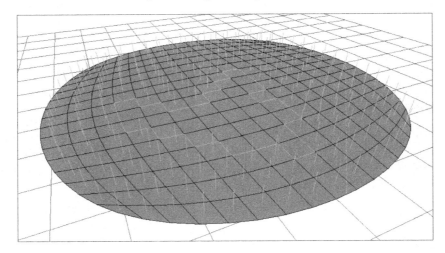

Now we will check the dragon for bad contiguous edges and eliminate the problem. If this is not fixed, the solidify modifier in the next chapter will not work properly:

1. Click on the **Solid** button again. Select the **Bad Contig. Edges:** button and see orange lines snaking around the dragon. This means that some of the normals on the dragon are pointing in the wrong direction. These polygons are facing towards the inside of the dragon, not the outside.

2. You can display all the normals by going to the **Mesh Display** subpanel of the 3D View Properties panel. Click on the polygon symbol under the label **Normals:** so that it is darkened. Set the **Size:** to **0.1mm**. If you set the 3D View shading to **Solid** and set the limit selection to visible button, it will be easier to see which way the normals point. You can see that the polygons within the edges identified by the **Bad Contig. Edges:** point a different way than the ones outside the edges.

3. Press *A* to select all the polygons.

4. Scroll up in the 3D **View** toolbox and find the buttons under the **Normals:** heading. Click on **Recalculate**.

5. Click on the **Solid** button in the **Print3D** subpanel.

Look at the results for **Bad Contig. Edges:**. It should be 0 now. When you finally apply the **Mirror** modifier, the dragon will be watertight and manifold. Well done.

Typical problem areas with a model

There are other problems your model may have, which can also prevent it from being able to be printed by a 3D printer. They are as follows:

- **Degenerate geometry**: With faces that have no area and edges that have no length, these can often be fixed with the **Remove Doubles** command

- **Distorted geometry**: It has faces that are not flat

- **Improper thickness**: It has walls that are too thin

- **Too sharp**: It has edges that are too sharp, and will not print correctly, or the object may break during or after printing because it is too thin and fragile

- **Too much overhang**: It has polygons that do not have proper support and may sag, or break during printing on some printers

We will explore ways to fix these in this chapter and the next.

Fixing distorted polygons

A distorted polygon is one that is not flat. A 3D printer may or may not have a problem with this. Following are the three things you can do with a distorted polygon:

- Flatten it

- Turn it into triangles because triangles are always flat

- Leave it alone and hope

When you export a Blender object to an STL file, the object gets triangulated automatically, so the distorted polygons are fixed, but the computer may not fix it the way you prefer. When you export a Blender object to an X3D file to make a textured object, the object is not triangulated.

Now, we'll examine the dragon for distorted polygons and see some of the things that we can do to fix them as follows:

1. Turn off the normals display in the **Mesh Display** subpanel of the 3D View window Properties panel so you can see the dragon better.

2. Click on the **Distorted** button in the **Checks:** section of the **Print3D** panel.

3. Select the **Non-Flat Faces:** button in the **Output:** section of the **Print3D** panel. Note that it shows **14** nonflat polygons.

4. Select the highlighted polygon on the dragon's arm as seen in the following screenshot:

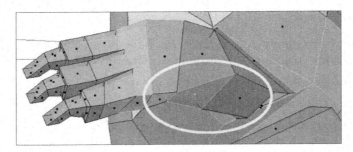

5. Navigate to the **Transform Orientation** button in the 3D View header. Change it from **Local** or **Global** to **Normal**. Notice how the 3D Manipulator icon over the chosen polygon rotates when you switch to normal. When it is set to **Normal**, you can see that the Z axis points directly away from the surface of the polygon. The Z axis is now the same as the normal and indicates a ray pointing perpendicular to the surface of the polygon. Now any changes you make in the polygon will be done with respect to the polygon's normal.

6. To flatten the polygon, press *S Z Z 0 Enter*. The letter *S* is for scale. Pressing *Z* twice tells Blender that you are not scaling in the global Z axis but in the local Z axis, and *0* says to scale it to zero. *Enter* executes the command.

7. Click on the **Distorted** button again. Note that the **Non-Flat Faces** button now shows only 13 distorted faces. When you click on it, that polygon is no longer highlighted.

8. Rotate the view so you can see under the dragon. There is a polygon at the bottom of the dragon's arm, highlighted as shown in the following screenshot. Fix it in the same way you just fixed the first polygon:

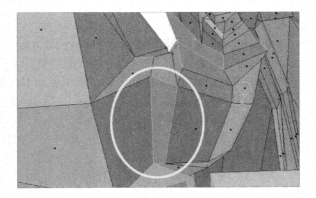

9. Click on the **Distorted** button again. Note that the **Non-Flat Faces** button now shows only 12 distorted faces. The polygon that you flattened is no longer highlighted.

10. Now, rotate your view of the dragon so that you can see the head. There is a distorted polygon in between the horns, as seen in the following screenshot:

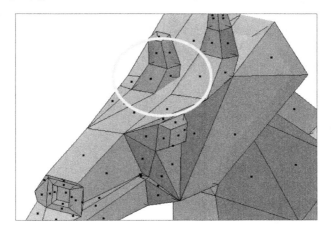

11. Get into vertex select mode. Choose the rear vertex at the base of the horn. Press *1* from the numpad to get the front view in the 3D View window.

12. In the **Preferences** panel of the 3D View, scroll down and check the **Mesh Analysis** checkbox. Set **Type:** to **Distortion** and the range from **45** to **90** degrees.

13. Distortion means that the polygon is not flat. The bending is measured in degrees. Below the lower value, the polygon is just displayed as a grey polygon. The lower number refers to the minimum distortion that the **Mesh Analysis** panel will display as distortion. The higher number refers to the maximum level of distortion that will be displayed. Any distortion greater than or equal to this number will also be displayed as red. This lets you set the upper and lower limits to search for a particular extent of distortion. In this case, I have allowed distortion below 45 degrees, and am tracking up to 90 degrees of distortion.

14. Move the vertex down and to the left as seen in the following screenshot. Use the color changes provided by the **Mesh Analysis** panel as your guide. You can move it to where the distortion is less than 45 degrees:

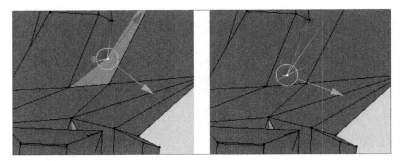

15. Uncheck the checkbox in the **Mesh Analysis** display subpanel.

16. Click on the **Distorted** button in the 3D View toolbox again. Note that the **Non-Flat Faces:** button now shows only ten distorted faces. When you click on it, that polygon is no longer highlighted.

17. Rotate the dragon so that you can see its side as shown in the following screenshot:

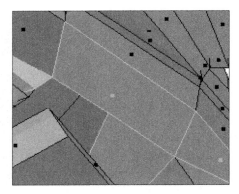

18. Select the largest highlighted polygon seen in the preceding screenshot. Scroll up in the 3D View toolbox and select **Deform: Smooth Vertex** in the **Mesh Tools** subpanel.

19. Click on the **Distorted** button in the **Print3D** toolbox again. Note that the **Non-Flat Faces:** button now shows only seven distorted faces. When you click on it, that polygon is no longer highlighted.

20. Save your file to a unique name.

We've used several methods to smooth out distorted faces. These include scaling to zero along the normal of the face, moving individual vertices with the **Mesh Analysis** tool to guide us, and using the **Smooth Vertex** tool. There is no best method as sometimes smoothing one face will distort the surrounding ones more. And, as you saw in the last exercise, smoothing one may also smooth the ones surrounding it.

The **Print3D** toolkit does have one cure-all for distorted faces, pressing the **Distorted** button in the **Cleanup:** section will triangulate all the faces of the object and eliminate any distortion. However, our dragon uses the **Subsurface** modifier. The vertices we are working with now are the control vertices for the final surface. So, we won't triangulate the faces just now.

Blunting sharp edges

Sharp edges are pretty obvious. You know them when you see them. Sometimes they are okay to print, sometimes they are not. The problem is that the thinness of the material at the edge may allow the part to break in printing, shipping, or use. So, how sharp is acceptable depends on what material you select and how thick your material is. Stainless steel holds a better edge than sandstone. Some plastics hold finer detail than stainless steel.

There are two kinds of sharp features on an object, long thin edges and points. Let's examine an object that has both of these and complements our dragon well, a sword:

1. Press the *Tab* key to get into Object mode. Select the fifth layer. Press *Home* to zoom in.

2. Select the sword. Press the *Tab* key to get into Edit mode. The vertices of the hilt are all hidden to make working on the blade easier. Make sure that the limit selection to visible setting is off and its button is light grey.

3. Press *Ctrl + 7* on the numpad to see the blade from the bottom and zoom in so that the blade fills the window.

4. Scroll down to the **Mesh Analysis** subpanel in the 3D View window Properties panel. Check the **Mesh Analysis** checkbox. Select the **Type:** button to **Sharp**. Set the lower limit to 20 degrees and the upper limit to 90 degrees.

The lower limit of the **Mesh Analysis** button's **Sharp Type:** tracks the minimum angle that you are declaring to be a sharp edge. The upper limit is the largest angle you want to track. The difference between distortion and sharpness is that distortion is an angle of folding within a polygon. Sharpness is folding between two polygons. One thing that may be counter intuitive is that a 20 degree angle is a sharper angle than a 90 degree angle. But remember that a 180 degree angle is a straight line. 90 degrees is a right angle.

As you have probably guessed, the tip of the blade and the edges are the sharpest parts. They appear red as in the top of the following screenshot. So, the angle is about 20 degrees at the edges. Rotate the view a little so you can see the tip of the blade and the edges.

The edges of the fuller, which is the depression in the center of the blade, are blue because there is a greater angle between them and the fuller, in contrast to the gentle angles within the fuller which show up in grey as seen at the bottom of the following screenshot:

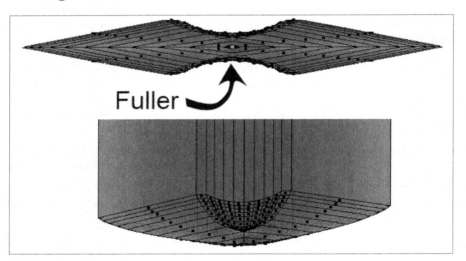

1. Press *Ctrl + 7* on the numpad again to see the base end of the blade. Use the **Ruler/Protractor** tool to measure the thickness of the blade from top to bottom, on either side of the fuller.

The thickness is about 0.44 mm. According to the specs for printing in nylon, the minimum thickness is 0.7 mm. So, this blade is going to need to be thicker. And it would be good if it was less sharp so that the edge of the blade is stronger. But, we still want a bit of a sharp edge just for looks. What we need to do is to make the fuller wide enough so that the blade will be strong. We will make it 0.9 mm thick. Then, we need to make the edge of the blade thick enough to be relatively strong, and add a point to the edge so it at least looks sharp.

2. Press *Esc* to get out of the **Ruler/Protractor** tool. Press the *Tab* key to go into object mode, press *A* to deselect the blade. Press *Shift + S* and select **Cursor to Center**.

3. Now press *Shift + A* and make a cube. Make the cube 0.9 mm x 0.9 mm x 0.9 mm in size. This is just a little larger than the minimum thickness. You can type in the values in the **Transform** subpanel of the 3D View window Properties panel. Then, select the blade again and go back into Edit mode. You can see the cube as a size reference for the blade.

4. Go into Edge Select mode and press the *Alt* key while selecting the edge of the blade. You want to select the entire edge where the blade is the sharpest.

5. Press *V*, and then *Enter* to rip the central edge into two separate edges.

6. Switch to Face Select mode. Press *B* and use the border select to select all the edges of the upper half of the blade. There are a couple of small polygons right at the tip of the blade so be sure to get them. Zoom in after selecting to make sure that you have selected them.

7. Press *G Y* and move the top half up so the top of the upper fuller is level with the top of the reference cube. You will see to two edges still connected from the top half. Don't worry about them.

8. Now select the faces of the bottom half and move them down until the bottom of the lower fuller is level with the bottom of the reference cube, as seen in the following screenshot:

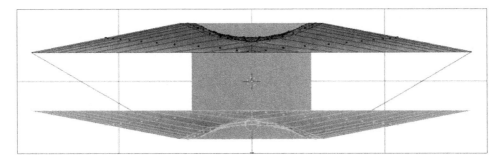

9. Next, select the two edges that go between the top half and the bottom half and delete them.

10. Select the bottom edge of the upper half of the blade with *Alt* + RMB. Then select the top edge of the lower half of the blade with *Shift* + *Alt* + RMB.

11. Choose **Mesh** on the View3D header then select **Edges | Bridge Edge Loops** from the pop-up menus.

12. Select all the vertical edges you have just made by moving the cursor over one and pressing *Ctrl* + *Alt* + RMB.

13. Press *W* and choose **Subdivide** from the pop-up menu.

14. Press *Shift* + *S* and select **Cursor to Center**, and then set the pivot point to **3D Cursor**.

15. Select all the edges of the blade's new center edge with *Alt* + RMB.

16. Press *S X* and move the edge out so the new sides of the edge are at about 45 degrees as seen in the following screenshot. If you scale it much wider, you will notice the edges of the sword turn red Press the LMB when done:

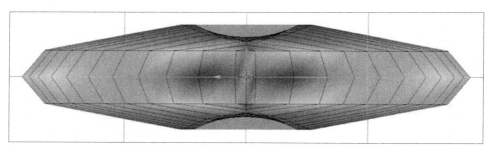

Now, as you can see in the preceding screenshot, some of the fuller is still not as wide as the reference cube that you made. This is okay. We made the reference cube a little larger than the minimum thickness for nylon. You can use the **Ruler/ Protractor** tool and the width of the narrowest part of fuller should be just under 0.7 mm. It shouldn't be a problem because the fuller was invented specifically to make a real sword lighter without sacrificing strength. The material on either side of the fuller is thick enough, and we have taken the edge and made it thicker and blunter, so it should be strong enough as well.

Fixing the junction between blade and hilt

Now we've made the blade wider but not the hilt. We should go and look at where they join and patch up any problems, as follows:

1. Press *1* on the numpad, and then *Home* to display the entire length of the sword.

2. Press *Alt + H* to show the hilt, or go to the 3D View header, select **Mesh | Show/Hide | Show Hidden** from the pop-up menus.

3. Press *Z* to select solid shading. Turn limit selection to visible on. Uncheck the **Mesh Analysis** checkbox.

4. Select an edge on the hilt next to the blade. Press . on the numpad to center on that edge.

5. Rotate the sword so you can see the junction of the blade and the hilt.

6. There are a few problems visible. The new edges you made for the blade are not attached to the hilt. The edges of the hilt are only attached to one side of the blade, so we need to go in and clean that up. It's not difficult.

7. Change to Face Select mode. Select the four faces as shown on the left side of the following screenshot. Delete them:

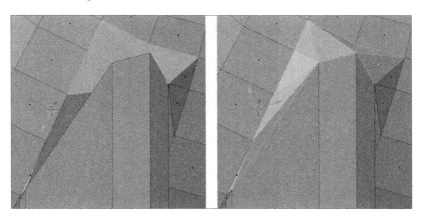

8. Rebuild the junction of the blade and hilt similar to the faces on the right side of the preceding screenshot.

9. Rotate the sword so you can see the other side of the blade. Repeat rebuilding the junction between the blade and the hilt.

10. Now switch on the Mesh Analysis button again. You can see, as shown in the following screenshot, that the sharpness is now confined to the new edge that you just built rather than the whole blade except the fuller:

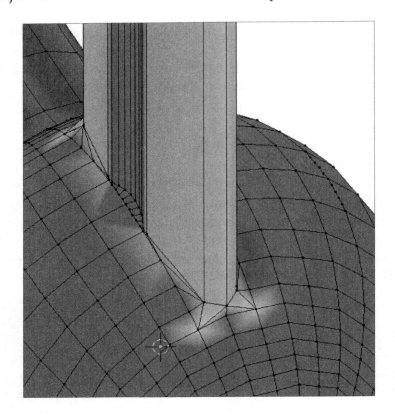

11. Use the **Print3D** subpanel to ensure that the sword is watertight and manifold. Save the file.

Economizing when 3D printing

In making the sword, we were introduced to the importance of making an object thick enough so it doesn't break. But that is not all that we need to be concerned with. The thicker the object is, the more material it requires. If the printer is charging by the material used, this can be a major consideration. I submitted the dragon to a 3D printing service several times during the building process. The initial dragon model was solid and it would have cost 224 percent as much to print as the final version where the body was hollowed out using **Solidify** and a well for the pen cup was created.

It also pays to shop around. Some local printers may charge you only 20 percent of what a national printer might. But they might not have the temperature controlled printer rooms and paid maintenance engineers. So, you need to see what works for you.

Blender has some tools to help you calculate the cost in the **3D Print** toolbox:

1. Look at the top of the **3D Print** toolbox. Look at the top two buttons, named **Volume:** and **Area:**.

2. Click on the **Volume:** button. At the bottom of the **Print3D** toolbox, there is a read-out for the **Volume:** button of the sword. The volume is about 0.453 cubic cm.

If the printer's price is $1.4 per cubic cm, the sword would cost about $0.63 to print, plus a service charge for setup and so on, and shipping. If the printer charges by the area, you can check that as well.

3D printing is an art. You may have to make changes to your model or rebuild it entirely with an eye to bringing the price down. With the lunar lander in *Chapter 1, Designing Objects for 3D Printing*, this included steps, such as modeling all of the fuel tanks as a single unit instead of individual cylinders. This removed the extra walls in the center of all the tanks. But each cylinder also had a hole punched in the bottom, which facilitated emptying out the extra printing material, but also took less material. The landing pad was changed from a solid block and material was removed from the bottom so it was more like a soda crate turned upside down. The rocket motors were also rebuilt as hollow objects and the framework holding the motors was changed from a series of cylinders to single circles extruded along paths to make smoother objects.

Summary

In this chapter, you were introduced to the **3D Print** toolbox and **Mesh Analysis** panel. You have learned how to make a model watertight and manifold so that it will print properly. Distorted polygons and sharp edges shouldn't be a problem for you anymore. You found out how to control the costs of 3D printing by minimizing the volume of the material in the model.

In the next chapter, you will discover proper building techniques to make a model strong, light, and precise. You will learn how to deal with overhanging polygons, reorient your object if needed, and how to output the file in STL and X3D formats.

4

Making Strong, Light Objects
with the Solidify Modifier

You have started building an object for 3D printing. You were introduced to the 3D Print Toolbox and the Mesh Analysis panel. You learned how to make objects watertight and manifold and fix any problems with the polygons. Now, it's time to complete the object by making it strong and light using the **Solidify modifier** and cleaning up the model. You will also learn about doing precision modeling, dealing with overhangs, and finally you will learn how to export the completed file.

We'll be covering the following topics in this chapter:

- Optimizing wall thickness
- Making an object hollow using the Solidify command
- Precision modeling — fitting two objects together
- Dealing with overhangs and support
- Exporting to STL and X3D

Optimizing wall thickness

Objects made with 3D printing are all subject to gravity. Failure to take this into consideration will result in objects that break or droop. We already worked a little with that in remodeling the sword, but it's time to take a more in-depth look.

The first thing to do is to find out the minimum wall thickness specifications for the material you will be printing in. You can find this information on the Web. It differs for each material. For the dragon, which will be printed in gypsum/sandstone, the minimum thickness is 2 mm for a supported wall and 3 mm for a freestanding wall.

Using Solidify for proper wall thickness

Now it's time to work with the dragon again. It's big, and so we need to do what we can to decrease its volume and reduce the cost. To do that, we will use a modifier called Solidify. What Solidify does is make a second wall parallel to the original wall, but at an offset. It does a good job, especially on simple objects. But our dragon is pretty complex, with thick and thin parts. So, we are going to have to clean up the model after finishing the Solidify operation.

In these following steps, we will investigate the Solidify modifier, apply it, and separate the inner wall we have just created from the original outer wall:

1. Open up the dragon file you were working on in the last chapter. Press *Tab* to get into Object mode. Select Layer 1 and the dragon.

2. Rotate the view so you can see the front and side of the dragon and center the dragon within the view so you can see it well. In the Blender Properties panel, select the **Modifiers** button in the header.

3. Check the eye button for the **Solidify modifier**. Suddenly, the dragon looks like it got attacked by a delirious cubist sculptor.

4. Whatever that is, it must be wrong. Open the **Solidify modifier** subpanel and check **Thickness:**. Is it set to **2 mm**? Hmmm, that can't be the problem then. Let's figure this out.

5. Scroll up in the **3D View** window and scroll the **Properties** panel up until you can see what the **Scale:** of the dragon is. **10**; there's the problem. The modifier is getting scaled as well as the object, so it's really giving the Solidify command a thickness of 20 mm, and not 2 mm. It's good that this was caught now. When you export a model for 3D printing, its scale must be at 1, 1, 1 or you will have problems getting the printer to print it at the proper size.

6. So, press *Ctrl + A* or select **Object** in the **3D View** header and navigate to **Apply | Scale** in the pop-up menus.

7. Now the size of the dragon is the same, but the scaling is 1, 1, 1 and the dragon looks better.

8. Rotate your view of the dragon counter-clockwise and you can see that it has a thickness inside.

9. We need two separate shells, not a solid object. One shell will become the inner surface. The other will become the outer surface. When they are finished and joined back together, they will define a solid shape with walls about 2 mm thick, but it is hollow in the center, like a ceramic vase. So look at the **Solidify modifier** panel and look at the bottom. Uncheck the **Fill Rim** checkbox. Now there are two separate surfaces.

10. Press the **Apply** button in the **Solidify modifier** panel.

11. We need to work on the inner shell, so switch to **Edit Mode**. Then choose **Mesh** from the header of the **3D View** window and navigate to **Vertices | Separate | By Loose Parts** from the pop-up menus.

12. Return to **Object Mode**. Press Z to change to wireframe shading in the **3D View**.

13. Select the inner shell.

Analyzing and modifying the inner shell

Now, we must plan what to do to the inner shell of the dragon to prepare it for use as the inner wall of the dragon's body:

- The wing is like an unsupported wall and is pretty large. So, it should be removed from the inner shell to give the greatest strength to the wing of the outer shell.

- The rear foot will be a supporting structure, so it should be strong. It will be removed from the inner shell and the calf is scaled down to strengthen it.

- The front paw is a very large unsupported structure. For the best strength, it will be removed from the inner shell.

- The head has problems; the nose pokes backwards through the outer shell. The horns need all the thickness they can get for strength, so the inner horns must go. The neck, because it will have to support so much weight, must be made thicker.

- The tail needs some rebuilding.

So, let's get started in fixing up the inner shell. We need to prepare the shell so we can see what we are doing better by giving it a different material than we used for the outer shell:

1. Just to be sure that nothing gets missed, press the Z key to return to solid shading.

2. In the **Properties** panel, choose the **Materials** button and open the **Materials** panel.

3. Click on the minus button to the right-hand side of where it says **Dragon Skin** to delete that material.

4. Press the **New** button below that to make a new texture. Name it Dragon Guts and set the Diffuse color as R = 0.224, G = 0.58, and B = 0.00. It is the color selected for the dragon's body in the second chapter. Then, set the **Specular Intensity** to 0.

5. Now rotate the view and you can see the inner shell and the outer shell. The inner shell is green, but there are a few places where they intersect and you can see the grey of the outer shell. We will have to fix this.

6. Select the outer shell of the dragon and press *M* to move it to layer 12.

7. Make only layer 1 visible. Press *Z* to return to wireframe mode. Press *3* on the numpad to get the side view.

The first thing to do to the inner shell of the dragon is to remove the foot and narrow down the calf so the foot can be a load bearing structure as given in the following steps:

1. Select the inner shell of the dragon. Go into **Edit Mode** and choose **Vertex Select**. Deselect all the vertices and press *Shift* + RMB to select all the vertices of the top of the foot as seen in the following screenshot:

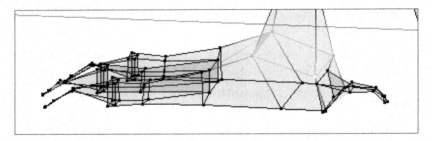

2. Press *X* to delete them. Select **Vertices** from the pop-up menu.

3. Select any vertex on the foot. Press *L*, which selects linked vertices, to select all the other vertices on the foot. Press *X* to delete them.

4. Rotate your view so you are looking up at the stump.

5. Press *Alt* + RMB and select the four vertices at the bottom of the stump. Press *F* to make a face on it.

6. Press *Alt* + RMB and select the edge loop above the stump. Set the pivot point to **Median Point**, press *S*, and make the calf of the leg narrower.

Next, the inner paw needs to be removed entirely so that the paw will be as strong as possible since it is entirely unsupported. This is illustrated as follows:

1. Pan up to the paw.

2. Select the edge loop, one loop from the body, as seen in the following screenshot:

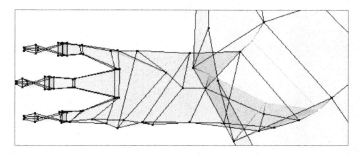

3. Press *X* to delete the vertices and eliminate the paw as you eliminated the foot.

4. Select the edges of the hole where the arm used to be by selecting an edge of the hole by pressing *Alt + RMB*.

5. Press *E Enter* and then *S 0 Enter*. Then press *W* and choose **Remove Doubles** from the pop-up menu. This extrudes a face, scales it to zero, and removes the extra vertices. It's a handy generic way of cleaning up areas of an inner shell.

Now, the wing must be removed from the inner shell. This is similar to removing the paw. This is illustrated as follows:

1. Rotate your view so you can see the wing from the side, as shown in the following screenshot:

2. By pressing *Alt* + RMB, select the edge loop at the dragon's elbow as seen in the preceding screenshot.

3. Eliminate the wing as you eliminated the foot and paw.

4. Next, select the five vertices as shown in the following screenshot and delete them:

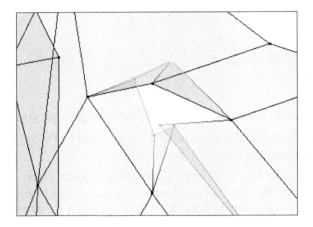

5. Next, by pressing *Alt* + RMB, select the edges on the perimeter of the hole you have created as seen in the following screenshot:

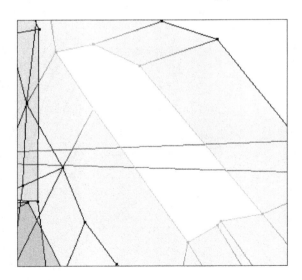

6. Press *E Enter* and then *S 0 Enter*. Then press *W* and choose **Remove Doubles** from the pop-up menu.

Next, it's time to work on the dragon's head. I mentioned that the nose was a problem, so it will have to be removed. This is illustrated as follows:

1. Press *3* on the numpad and pan the view so you can see the dragon's head.

2. Delete the dragon's horns and fill the holes.

3. Press *Ctrl + 3* on the numpad to get the Left Ortho view. Deselect all faces.

4. Move the cursor just above and to the left of the nose. Press *K* and move the knife tool down with the mouse while holding down the LMB. This shows where the cuts to the faces of the snout will be, as seen on the left-hand side of the following screenshot. Let go of the LMB and then click on the LMB again. Then press *Enter* to complete the cut.

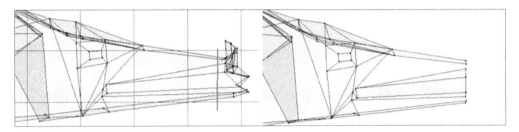

5. Deselect all vertices and then press *B* and use the border select to choose all of the vertices to the right of the ones you just cut. Delete them as seen on the right-hand side of the preceding screenshot.

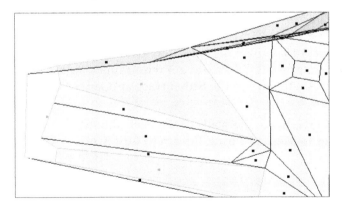

6. Rotate the view so you can see the other side of the dragon's head. Fill in the holes in its upper and lower snout. Make a polygon to cap the end of its snout as seen in the preceding screenshot.

7. Go into **Object Mode**. Display layers 1 and 12. Set the **Viewport Shading** to **Solid**. Inspect the head.

8. There seems to be two places where the inner shell appears through the outer shell as seen in the following screenshot:

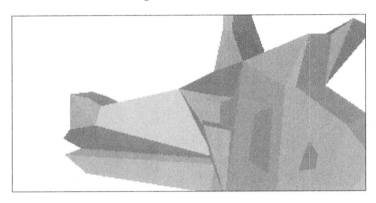

9. This shouldn't be. Press *Z* to get wireframe shading. Rotate your view around the dragon's head. See if you can see what the problem is.

10. I can't see any problem.

11. The two shells don't appear to conflict. Open the **Modifiers** panel in the **Properties** panel. Darken the eye in the **Subsurface modifier** subpanel.

12. Select the outer shell and do the same.

13. Press *Z* to get solid shading. Inspect the dragon again. It looks good. So, there shouldn't be a problem after everything is done.

14. Select Layer 1 to display only the inner shell of the dragon once more. Select the inner shell. Press *Z* to get wireframe shading and in the **Properties** panel, click on the eye in the **Subsurface** subpanel to turn the **Subsurface modifier** off.

15. To support the head, the walls of the neck should be extra thick. Set the pivot point to **Median Point**. Return to **Edit Mode**.

16. Press *Alt* + RMB and select the first edge loop in the neck, as shown in the following screenshot. Press *S 0.6 Enter*. This scales the neck to 6/10ths of its former size:

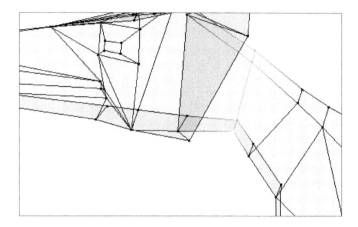

17. Repeat this for the other two edge loops in the neck.

The tail needs a little work. The geometry needs to be smoothed out a bit. Look at the left-hand side of the following screenshot and you will see that there seems to be a valley in the tail instead of it being nicely rounded. The right-hand side of the following screenshot shows a couple of vertices on the very tip of the tail that need to be moved to the left so that they are the same side of the x axis as the rest of the model.

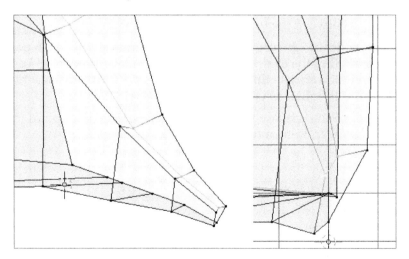

1. Press *Ctrl + 1* on the numpad to get the back view. Zoom into the tail.

2. For each of the four vertices highlighted in the left of the preceding screenshot, select it and move it up a little to make a decent curve as shown on the right-hand side of the screenshot.

3. Select the two vertices at the end of the tail, highlighted on the right-hand side of the preceding screenshot, and move them so they are both to the left of center.

4. The second vertex from the right on the bottom of the dragon is a little low. Move it up in line with the others.

5. Press *Home* and rotate the view so you can see the open side of the dragon.

6. Select all the edges on the open side of the dragon with *Alt* + RMB.

7. Press *Shift + S* and choose **Cursor to Center**. Set the pivot point to **3D Cursor**. Press *S X 0 Enter*. Now that edge is snapped to the center in the x axis.

8. Now it's time to do a final check on the inner and outer shells of the dragon.

9. Switch to **Object Mode**. Make both Layer 1 and Layer 12 visible. Make the **Subsurface modifier** of both shells visible. Press *Z* to switch to solid shading.

10. Inspect the dragon and make sure that the inner shell does not penetrate the outer shell. Notice the gap between the shells in the neck area. It's thicker so the neck will be stronger, but there is plenty of room in the inner neck so any excess material inside the head can be shaken out.

11. Press *Z* to enter wireframe mode, select the inner shell and note the differences between the two models. You've done well.

12. As a precaution, to ensure that the mirror operation will work perfectly on the outer shell of the dragon, select the outer shell of the dragon, go into **Edit Mode**, and then choose **Edge Select**. Press *Alt* + RMB and select the center perimeter of the shell as you did for the inner shell.

13. Press *Shift + S* and choose **Cursor to Center**. Set the pivot point to **3D Cursor**. Press *S X 0 Enter*. Return to **Object Mode**. Save the file.

Now it's time to put things together. This is illustrated as follows:

1. Select the dragon's inner shell. Open the modifications panel of the **Properties** panel. Make the **Mirror modifier** visible. Apply the **Mirror modifier**.

2. Make the **Subsurface modifier** visible. Apply the **Subsurface modifier**.

3. Select the dragon's outer shell. Repeat what you did to the inner shell.

4. Inspect the two shells.

5. Use the **Print 3D Toolbox** to double check that the shells are solid and manifold.

6. Make sure that Layer 1, Layer 12, and Layer 20 are turned on. Press *F12* to render the dragon. It should look just like it did in *Chapter 2, Measuring and Texturing Techniques for 3D Printing*.

7. Save the file to a unique name.

Making the dragon useful

Your dragon is beautiful. Now it is time to make it useful and stick a pencil cup in its back:

1. Press the *Esc* key to return to the **3D View** in the largest window. Display only Layer 1.

2. Select the dragon's inner shell. Go into **Edit Mode**. In the **Mesh Display** subpanel, click on the **display face normals as lines** button. A normal shows you which direction a polygon is facing. Make sure that all the normals are facing outward and that the blue lines used to represent them extend past the inner shell. If they are not, select all the edges and use the **Recalculate** button in the Tool Shelf. If the normals are not facing outward, the next step will not work right.

3. Return to **Object Mode**. Open up the **Boolean modifier** subpanel. Booleans are very powerful modifiers. They allow you to control the shape of one object with another object. Here, we are going to use the Boolean modifier to put a complex depression into the back of the dragon. If you want an in-depth explanation of Boolean operations, check *Chapter 8, Making the Sloop* of *Blender 3D Basics*.

4. For the Object, select **Pen Cup Boolean Inner Shell**. Choose **Intersect** as the **Operation:**. Click on the eye button so you can see the Boolean operation. It should look like the following screenshot:

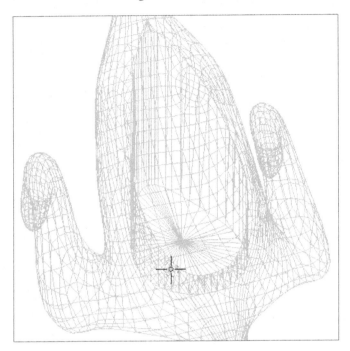

5. Go to Layer 12. Select the dragon's outer shell. Once again, make sure that the normals are facing outwards.

6. Return to **Object Mode**. Open up the **Boolean modifier** subpanel. Choose **Pen Cup Boolean Outer Shell** as the **Object**. Choose **Intersect** as the **Operation:**. Click on the eye so you can see the Boolean operation.

7. If they both look good, apply the **Boolean modifier** to the outer shell. Then go to Layer 1 and apply the **Boolean** to the inner shell.

8. Press the *Tab* key to go to **Edit Mode**. In the Tool Shelf, select **Normals: Flip Direction**. This will be the inner section of the body, so the normals must point towards the inside instead of the outside as they usually do.

9. Save the file so you have a version for a material extrusion printer.

Cutting holes for removing extra printing material

If you are using a printer that uses a powder or liquid for material, you will need to cut holes out of the bottom so that the extra material can be removed. This is not necessary if you are using material extrusion printing like most hobbyist printers:

1. Return to **Object Mode**. Press *Ctrl + 7* on the numpad. Display layer 12. Select the outer shell. Set the **Shading** to **Solid**. Go to **Edit Mode**. Turn off the **Normals:** display. Display the faces.

2. The printing specification allows us one hole, two holes, or four holes. They are thinking of round holes. In the interest of time, we will make rectangular ones. But remember that stress-wise, round holes are much stronger.

> To make round holes, what you do is create a cylinder of the diameter of the holes you want. Line it up where the hole should be; make sure it does not extend up into the pencil cup but does extend below the dragon. Duplicate it, move the duplicate across the x axis, and join the cylinders into a single object.
>
> Select the outer shell, make a Boolean modifier, and choose the cylinders as the Boolean object. Use a difference operation, apply it, and then in the dragon, delete the vertices at the top of where the cylinder is inside the dragon. Repeat these steps with the inner shell, but delete the vertices at the bottom of where the cylinder meets the dragon. Then, you connect the holes in a similar manner to the way we connect the rectangular holes.
>
> This is what I did for the sample dragon shown at the end of the chapter.

3. For four holes, each hole should be 10 mm in diameter. Use the **Ruler / Protractor** to measure the width of the central polygons.

4. It turns out that each polygon is about 5 mm on a side. So, to be roughly equal to four 10 mm holes, we need to delete 16 polygons as seen in the following screenshot:

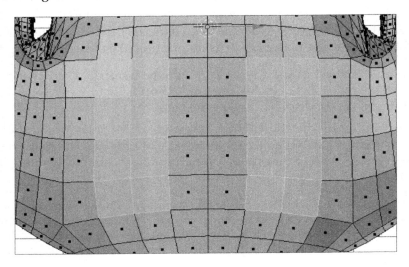

5. Select the faces and delete them.

6. Return to **Object Mode**. Display both Layer 1 and Layer 12. Select the inner shell and go to **Edit Mode**.

7. Delete the faces in the inner shell that correspond to the holes in the outer shell.

8. Go to **Object Mode**, press *Shift*, and select the outer shell as well as the inner shell.

9. Press *Ctrl + J* to join them. Then press *Tab* to return to **Edit Mode**.

10. Choose **Select Edges**. Press *Alt + RMB* and choose the edges that surround one hole of the inner shell. Press *Shift + Alt + RMB* and select the edges that surround that hole of the outer shell as well.

11. From the **3D View** header, choose **Mesh** and then navigate to **Edges | Bridge Edge Loops** from the pop-up menus. Repeat this with the other hole.

12. Check that the object is solid and manifold. Save your file.

13. Get into **Object Mode**. Turn on layers 12 and 20 to display your dragon and make the camera and lamp active. Do a test render to ensure that all your maps are in place.

Congratulations! Your dragon is done.

Precision modeling—fitting two objects together

As a bonus, a tower shaped pencil/pen cup has been provided in layer 6. It can be any material you prefer. But before you go and print it up, you want to make sure it will fit into the dragons back. The clearance specification for the material that the dragon is made from is 0.9 mm as seen in the following screenshot. This means that there should be a gap of at least 0.9 mm between the dragon and the tower if you want to be sure that they won't bind:

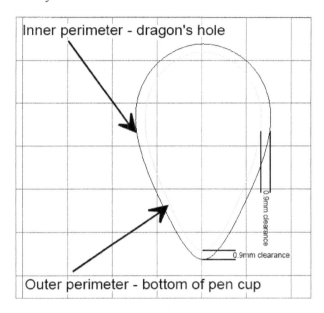

Inner perimeter - dragon's hole

0.9mm clearance

0.9mm clearance

Outer perimeter - bottom of pen cup

1. Get into wireframe mode. Use your measuring tools to check this. The easiest way in this case would be to just measure the outer width of the pencil cup at its bottom, and the inner width of the cavity in the dragon's back. Make sure that the width of the cavity is at least 1.8 mm (0.18 cm) larger than the width of the pencil cup. If they need to be modified, scale the pencil cup in X or Y as needed.

2. You can scale it in X or Y, then note the scale in the 3D View Properties panel, and scale the pencil cup to the same percentage in the other dimension.

3. Remember what you learned with the scaling of the dragon at the beginning of this chapter. Be sure to apply the scale to the object once it is the proper size. Other materials have different clearance specifications, and painting parts and other finishing techniques can also affect the clearance. Keep those factors in mind when sizing the tower. Save the file to a unique name.

Dealing with overhangs and support

Material extrusion printers that extrude a filament of plastic have one additional issue that most other printers do not, the issue of overhang. Other printers use the raw printing material to support the object, but material extrusion printers cannot. When the printer is printing a layer without another layer directly underneath, there will be nothing to support the plastic that is being laid down. A 45 degree angle is considered the maximum angle that is acceptable. When the material extrusion printer deposits the perimeter of a layer, often the perimeter is two extrusions wide as seen in the following screenshot. The inner perimeter is supported by the layer underneath and the outer perimeter is supported by the inner perimeter:

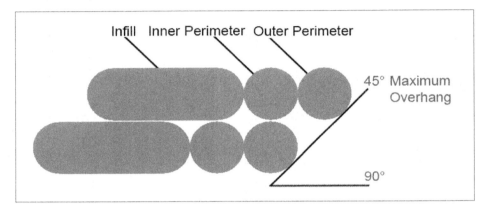

There are four solutions to this problem:

- Modifying your object so there is less overhang
- Finding an orientation for your object where there is no overhang; printing it upside down or on its side
- The slicers for some material extrusion printers automatically make a support when they detect an overhang
- Making your own supports

If the printer automatically makes supports

If you are using a material extrusion printer that automatically generates supports, here's how to finish your object:

1. Open the file you saved for a material extrusion printer. Go into **Object Mode**.

2. Select the inner shell then select the outer shell. Press *Ctrl + J* to join them.

3. Save the file to a unique name. You are ready to print.

Making supports for your model

If you have no other choice, then you must make supports for your model. This is not an exact science and you need to know what the printer you are using can do to span a gap between supports. Your dragon does not need holes in its bottom to shake out extra powder if you are using a material extrusion printer. Nor do material extrusion printers support textures; everything will be the same color:

1. Open the file you saved for a material extrusion printer. Go into **Object Mode**. Select the outer shell.

2. Change to **Solid View**. Go into **Edit Mode**. Deselect all of the edges. Turn off the **Normals:** display. Rotate the view so you can see the bottom of the dragon. Check the **Mesh Analysis** checkbox in the **3D View** properties panel. Set the **Type:** to **Overhang**. Set **limit the selection** to visible. The dragon will look similar to the following screenshot:

If you were making a support for the dragon, the **Mesh Analysis** would look like the preceding screenshot. The colored areas have all been flagged for needing support. The tail, bottom, and feet will all be on the printer bed, so they don't need to be supported. The belly, paws, and head do need support:

1. To build a support, first go into Face Select mode. Select a polygon that has been colored red by the **Mesh Analysis**, say under the dragon's chin. Press *I* to inset the face and then scale it down to about the smallest size you think the printer can print, as seen on the left-hand side of the following screenshot. This is to make the support easy to break off after you have printed it and minimize the sanding you will need to do.

2. Select the polygon in the center of the inset. Extrude it a little.

3. Set the pivot point to **Median Point**. Scale up the face to a size that you think can support the weight.

4. Extrude it again as seen on the right-hand side of the following screenshot. Press *Shift + S* and choose **Cursor to Center**. Set the pivot point to **3D Cursor**. Press *S Z 0 Enter* to make your support flat on the bottom and extend down to the printing bed.

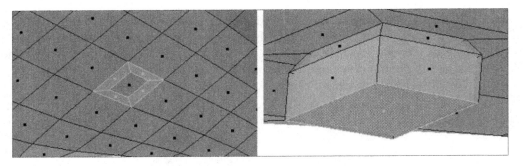

5. Now you have a support that goes all the way to the printing bed, as seen in the following screenshot. Make as many as you need to hold up the unsupported part of the object.

6. Go into **Object Mode**. Select Layer 1 as well as Layer 12. Select the inner shell as well as the outer shell. Press *Ctrl + J* to join them.

7. Save your file.

Exporting your 3D object

There are two kinds of files for exporting Blender objects to be printed in 3D; STL files and X3D files. A few 3D printer companies offer plugins that export Blender files to their website as well. STL files do not carry any color information. Your color comes from the color material that is chosen as I mentioned in *Chapter 1, Designing Objects for 3D Printing*. The pencil cup is an example of this. No material was ever specified. It takes its red color from the plastic chosen for printing. X3D files are really interactive 3D file formats; they carry color information and 3D printing bureaus accept them for printing.

When I am getting ready to export an STL or X3D file for 3D printing, I like to put the object(s) to be printed into their own layer of the Blender file, usually Layer 1.

Getting the orientation right

You've used Blender enough to be familiar with Blender's **Z-Up axes** as shown on the left-hand side of the following diagram:

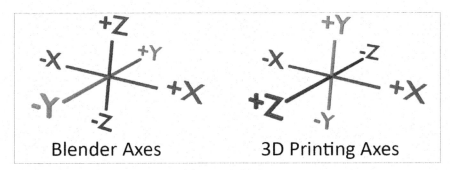

Many 3D printers use a **Y-Up** orientation as seen on the right-hand side of the preceding diagram. If the printer you are using is Y-Up orientation, you want to rotate your object 90 degrees in X before exporting it so it will be oriented correctly for printing. To be sure of how they orient their geometry, consult the printing service.

 An easy way to orient is to first select the object. Then, set the 3D cursor to center. Set the pivot point to 3D cursor. Press *R X 90 Enter* to rotate it.

Making an STL file

STL files do not have any color or texture information. They make all the polygons into triangles so you are guaranteed to have no distorted faces. The best way to double-check your STL file is to import your STL file back into Blender and see what you have. The STL export process will only export objects that are in a visible layer and selected. Unselected objects in a visible layer will not be exported, nor will anything in a hidden layer.

Making STL files is easy:

1. Select the object(s) that you want to print and make sure they are visible. The STL export process will only export objects that are in a visible layer and selected. Unselected objects in a visible layer will not be exported, nor will anything in a hidden layer.

2. Select **File** at the top of the **Blender** window. Choose **Export** and **STL** from the drop-down menus.

3. Select a name for the STL file then click on the **Export STL** button in the upper-right of the window.

4. Follow the uploading directions on your printer's website.

Making an X3D file with a texture

X3D files do have color and texture information. The X3D exporter does not triangulate your polygons. All objects in visible layers will be exported. For X3D files, the printing bureau will want a ZIP file with both your object file and the graphics file you using for your texture. Blender does not combine the files and zip them up when it exports the file. You will have to do it. As stated in *Chapter 2, Measuring and Texturing Techniques for 3D Printing*, it is best to put the graphic file in the same folder as the Blender file. X3D files can be proofed either by importing them back in Blender or by using an X3D viewer available on the Internet:

1. Choose which layers are visible. Select **File** at the top of the **Blender** window.

2. Choose **Export** and **X3D Extensible** from the drop-down menus.

3. Select a name for the X3D file then click on the **Export X3D** button in the upper-right of the window.

4. Then put the `.x3d` and texture files into a zip file.

5. Follow the uploading directions on the bureau's website.

Summary

As seen in the preceding screenshot, this is what the dragon looks like when it returns from the printer. I customized it a little by coloring the eyes and giving them Anime style double highlights, but leaving the horns green, and I wanted to make the wings look as they are semi-transparent by showing the blood veins.

In this chapter, you discovered how to use the **Solidify modifier** to create a solid shell for the object and you learned proper building techniques to make a model strong, light, and precise. You learned how to make sure two objects will fit together correctly. You discovered how to deal with overhanging polygons, and how to output the file in STL and X3D formats. Congratulations and have fun doing 3D printing.

3D Printing References

As you continue learning about 3D printing, you may have questions about the capabilities of certain 3D printers or printing services, or want inspiration on what to make. These links should help you.

References

These are a variety of links I discovered while writing this book. They include communities of 3D printing enthusiasts and links to keep up with what's going on:

- **3Ders.org**: 3D printer and 3D printing news available at `http://www.3ders.org/index.html`
- **Case Western**: 3D printing design fails available at `https://docs.google.com/document/d/142LhI2XYRTBgERyJMcjWn-MIb5Txo20lFNfDYIFxzbM/view?pli=1`
- **Mashable**: 3D printing available at `http://mashable.com/category/3d-printing/`
- **Oddee**: 10 amazing 3D printed objects available at `http://www.oddee.com/item_98686.aspx`
- **Soliforum 3D printing community**: `http://www.soliforum.com/`
- **Top 3D printing sites on the web**: `http://www.3ders.org/stats/20121209-top-100-websites-2012-in-3d-printing-industry.html`
- **Blender Key Commands**: `http://waldobronchart.be/blenderkeyboard/`
- **Using Blender on a Macbook**: `http://devnulldb.blogspot.com/2012/07/using-blender-on-macbook.html`

3D printing services

The following are links to companies that create 3D printed objects from the models you submit:

- **Find a local 3D printer near you, the smaller services**: `http://www.makexyz.com/`

- **Design Anything.com**: Find custom figurines, awards, jewelry, and more available at `http://www.designanything3d.com/`

- **I.Materialize**: Find objects up to 6 feet in size, 70 materials available at `http://i.materialise.com/`

- **Moddler.com**: This is for industrial designers, fine artists, architects, and inventors available at `http://www.moddler.com/`

- **Ponoko**: 3D printing and laser cutting available at `http://www.ponoko.com/`

- **Redeye**: Service bureau for Stratasys available at `http://www.redeyeondemand.com`

- **Sculpteo**: This accepts Blender files directly available at `http://www.sculpteo.com/`

- **Shapeways**: To make, sell, and buy available at `http://www.shapeways.com/`

- **ZoomRP**: Emphasis on rapid available at `http://www.zoomrp.com/`

3D printers – hobbyist

The following is a list of 3D printers aimed at the 3D printing hobbyist. It's not intended to be inclusive because new 3D printers are springing up every day, but it includes the leaders as of now, and a few newcomers:

- **Afinia**: `http://www.afinia.com/3d-printers`
- **Airwolf**: `http://airwolf3d.com/`
- **Bukobot**: `http://bukobot.com/`
- **Cube**: `http://cubify.com/cube/`
- **Felix Printers**: `http://shop.felixprinters.com/`

- **Lulzbot**: http://www.lulzbot.com/
- **Makerbot**: http://www.makerbot.com/
- **Makergear**: http://www.makergear.com/
- **Mbot**: http://www.mbot3d.com/
- **Peachy Printer**: http://www.peachyprinter.com/
- **Printrbot**: http://printrbot.com/
- **Robo**: http://www.robo3dprinter.com/
- **Reprap**: http://reprap.org/wiki/RepRap
- **Solidoodle**: http://www.solidoodle.com/
- **Tinkerine Studio**: http://www.tinkerines.com/
- **Trinity Labs**: http://trinitylabs.com/
- **Type A Machines**: http://www.typeamachines.com/
- **Ultimaker**: https://www.ultimaker.com/
- **Up Mini**: http://www.up3dusa.com/#!up-mini/c1hlm
- **B9 Creator**: Liquid resin available at http://b9creator.com/
- **Form Labs**: Liquid resin available at http://formlabs.com/

3D printers – industrial

The industrial 3D printers are the high precision, high quality, and high price printers. But you can find a service that uses them and have the service make your object:

- **3D Systems**: http://www.3dsystems.com/
- **EnvisionTec**: http://envisiontec.com/3d-printers/
- **Made in Space**: http://www.madeinspace.us/
- **mCor Technologies**: http://www.mcortechnologies.com/
- **Stratasys**: http://www.stratasys.com/3d-printers

3D objects

Surely you want to make your objects yourself but sometimes it's good to have a little help in modeling, especially if you are on a deadline. There is no guarantee that the models listed are 3D printer-ready though:

- **60 sites with free 3D models**: http://www.blendernation. com/2009/03/23/60-sites-with-free-3d-models/
- **Blender Models.com**: http://www.blender-models.com/
- **Blendswap.com**: http://www.blendswap.com/
- **Next Wave Multimedia**: Free Blender models available at http://nextwavemultimedia.com/html/3dblendermodel.html
- **TF3DM free Blender models**: http://tf3dm.com/3d-models/blender
- **Thingiverse**: http://www.thingiverse.com/

Index

Symbols

1 button 22
3D objects
  60 sites with free 3D models 92
  Blender Models.com 92
  Blendswap.com 92
  exporting 85-87
  Next Wave Multimedia 92
  STL file, creating 86, 87
  TF3DM free Blender models 92
  Thingiverse 92
  X3D file, creating with texture 87
  Y-Up orientation 86
  Z-Up axes 86
3D printer
  controlling 11, 12
  parts 11
  types 9, 10
  working 7-9
3D printer, materials
  Acrylonitrile Butadiene Styrene (ABS) 15
  Aliphatic polyamide (nylon) 15
  LAYWOO-D3 16
  photopolymers 16
  Polyethylene terephthalate (PET) 15
  Polylactic acid (PLA) 15
3D printer, types
  Binder jetting 10
  Directed energy deposition 10
  Direct Metal Laser Sintering (DMLS) 10
  material extrusion 9
  material jetting 9
  Powder bed fusion 10

  Selective heat sintering (SHS) 10
  Selective Laser Sintering (SLS) 10
  sheet lamination printers 10
  Vat photopolymerization 10
3D printing
  about 5
  cost, calculating 64
  exercise 6
  features 45
  health effects 16
  hobbyist references 90
  manifold model, creating 50
  materials 15
  noncontiguous edges, fixing 53, 54
  references 89
  services 16, 90
  using, opportunities 6, 7
  watertight model, creating 49
3D printing hobbyist
  references 90
3D printing hobbyist references
  Afinia 90
  Airwolf 90
  B9 Creator 91
  Bukobot 90
  Cube 90
  Felix Printers 90
  Form Labs 91
  Lulzbot 91
  Makerbot 91
  Makergear 91
  Mbot 91
  Peachy Printer 91
  Printrbot 91

Reprap 91
Robo 91
Solidoodle 91
Tinkerine Studio 91
Trinity Labs 91
Type A Machines 91
Ultimake 91
Up Mini 91
3D printing references
3Ders.org 89
Blender Key Commands 89
Case Western 89
Mashable 89
Oddee 89
Soliforum 3D printing community 89
Using Blender on a Macbook 89
3D printing services
Design Anything.com 90
I.Materialize 90
Moddler.com 90
Ponoko 90
Redeye 90
Sculpteo 90
Shapeways 90
ZoomRP 90
3D Systems 91
60 sites with free 3D models
URL 92

A

Acrylonitrile Butadiene Styrene (ABS) 15
Afinia 90
Airwolf 90
Aliphatic polyamide (nylon) 15
Alt + RMB 62

B

B9 Creator 91
Bad Contig. Edges: button 54
binder jetting 10
Blender
precision modeling 19
setting up, for metric scaling 48, 49
texture painting 40

Blender Models.com
URL 92
Blendswap.com
URL 92
Bukobot 90

C

coloring model
preparing 26
texture map, painting 40
texture maps, building 28
Ctrl button 23
Ctrl + MMB (Middle Mouse Button) 33
Cube 90
Cube printing 11

D

Design Anything.com
URL 90
dimensions
modeling 13
Directed energy deposition 10
Direct Metal Laser Sintering (DMLS) 10
Distorted button 58
dragon
holes, cutting 79, 80
making, to use 77, 78
material extrusion printer, using 83
model support, creating 83, 84
overhang issue, dealing with 82
precision modelling 81

E

Electron Beam Melting (EBM). *See*
        Directed energy deposition
EnvisionTec 91
Export STL button 87

F

Felix Printers 90
file size 13
Form Labs 91
Fused Filament Fabrication (FFF). *See*
        material extrusion

G

G button 32
Granular Materials Binding. *See* **powder bed fusion**

H

Home key 20
hot end simulator 9

I

I.Materialize
  URL 90
industrial 3D printers
  3D Systems 91
  EnvisionTec 91
  Made in Space 91
  mCor Technologies 91
  Stratasys 91

L

LAYWOO-D3 16
LMB (Left Mouse Button) 22
Lulzbot 91

M

Made in Space 91
Makerbo 91
Makergear 91
manifold model
  conditions 50
  creating 50, 51
  manifold edges, identifying 51
  non manifold issues, searching 52, 53
material extrusion 9
material jetting 9
Mbot 91
mCor Technologies 91
MendelMaxPro 11
Mesh Analysis checkbox 63
Mesh Analysis panel 47
Mirror modifier 52

Moddler.com
  URL 90
model
  coloring, ways 26
  uncoloring 26
  vertex colors, applying 26, 27
  vertex painting 27
model issues
  blade and hilt junction, fixing 63
  degenerate geometry 55
  distorted geometry 55
  distorted polygons, fixing 55-58
  improper thickness 55
  overhang 55
  sharp edges, blunting 59-62
  sharpness 55
Molten Polymer Deposition (MPD). *See* **material extrusion**

N

Next Wave Multimedia
  URL 92
Non-Flat Faces button 57
Non Manifold Edges: button 53

O

object precision
  affecting, factors 14

P

Paint mode 41
Paint tool 40
Peachy printer 13, 91
photopolymer jetting. *See* **material jetting**
photopolymers 16
Polyethylene terephthalate (PET) 15
polygons sizes 14
Polylactic acid (PLA) 15
Ponoko
  URL 90
powder bed fusion 10

precision modeling, Blender
  about 19-21
  Ruler/Protractor, using 21-25
Preview window 28
Print3D Toolbox
  diagram 47
  installing 46
  location 47
printing costs
  controlling 14
Printrbot 91

R

R button 32
Redeye
  URL 90
Reprap 91
RMB (Right Mouse Button) 20
Robo 91
Ruler/Protractor
  about 60
  object thickness, measuring 25
  used, for angle measuring 24
  using 21-23

S

S button 32
Sculpteo
  URL 90
Selective heat sintering (SHS) 10
Selective Laser Melting (SLM) 10
Selective Laser Sintering (SLS) 10
Shapeways
  URL 90
sheet lamination printers 10
Shift + A 20
Shift + Alt + RMB 62
Shift + D Enter 20
slicing program 8
Smooth Vertex tool 59
Solidify modifier
  about 67
  inner shell, analysing 69-77
  inner shell, modifying 69-77
  used, for inner wall separation 68, 69

Solidoodle 91
stacking tolerances 24
stepper motors 11
Stereolithography (SLA). *See*
        Vat photopolymerization
Stratasys 91

T

Tab key 59
texture maps
  painting 40
  printing colors, selecting 28, 29
  UV Layout, exporting 40
  UV unwrapping 29
texture painting, Blender
  about 40, 41
  Clone brush, using 42, 43
  UV coordinates modification,
        for detail adding 41
TF3DM free Blender models
  URL 92
Thingiverse
  URL 92
Tinkerine Studio 91
tolerance 20
Transform Orientation button 56
Type A Machines 91

U

Ultimake 91
Up Mini 91
UV/Image Editor 39
UV unwrapping
  dragon's belly, mapping 35, 36
  head, UV mapping 38, 39
  UV maps, applying to wings 29-35
  wing edge, UV mapping 37, 38

V

Vat photopolymerization 10
V button 27
vertex painting 27
View mode 41
Volume: button 65

W

watertight model
  creating 49, 50

Y

Y-Up orientation 86

Z

ZoomRP
  URL 90
Z-Up axes 86

Thank you for buying
Blender 3D Printing Essentials

About Packt Publishing

Packt, pronounced 'packed', published its first book *"Mastering phpMyAdmin for Effective MySQL Management"* in April 2004 and subsequently continued to specialize in publishing highly focused books on specific technologies and solutions.

Our books and publications share the experiences of your fellow IT professionals in adapting and customizing today's systems, applications, and frameworks. Our solution based books give you the knowledge and power to customize the software and technologies you're using to get the job done. Packt books are more specific and less general than the IT books you have seen in the past. Our unique business model allows us to bring you more focused information, giving you more of what you need to know, and less of what you don't.

Packt is a modern, yet unique publishing company, which focuses on producing quality, cutting-edge books for communities of developers, administrators, and newbies alike. For more information, please visit our website: www.packtpub.com.

About Packt Open Source

In 2010, Packt launched two new brands, Packt Open Source and Packt Enterprise, in order to continue its focus on specialization. This book is part of the Packt Open Source brand, home to books published on software built around Open Source licences, and offering information to anybody from advanced developers to budding web designers. The Open Source brand also runs Packt's Open Source Royalty Scheme, by which Packt gives a royalty to each Open Source project about whose software a book is sold.

Writing for Packt

We welcome all inquiries from people who are interested in authoring. Book proposals should be sent to author@packtpub.com. If your book idea is still at an early stage and you would like to discuss it first before writing a formal book proposal, contact us; one of our commissioning editors will get in touch with you.

We're not just looking for published authors; if you have strong technical skills but no writing experience, our experienced editors can help you develop a writing career, or simply get some additional reward for your expertise.

3D Printing Blueprints

ISBN: 978-1-84969-708-8   Paperback: 310 pages

Installation and Administration

1. Design 3D models that will print successfully using Blender, a free 3D modelling program

2. Customize, edit, repair, and then share your creations on Makerbot's Thingiverse website

3. Easy-to-follow guide on 3D printing; learn to create a new model at the end of each chapter

Blender 3D Architecture, Buildings, and Scenery

ISBN: 978-1-84719-367-4   Paperback: 332 pages

Reclaiming Productivity for faster Java Web Development

1. Turn your architectural plans into a model

2. Study modeling, materials, textures, and light basics in Blender

3. Create photo-realistic images in detail

4. Create realistic virtual tours of buildings and scenes

Please check **www.PacktPub.com** for information on our titles

Blender 2.6 Cycles: Materials and Textures Cookbook

ISBN: 978-1-78216-130-1   Paperback: 280 pages

Installation and Administration

1. Create a basic Cycles material mixing the closure components

2. Connect nodes of different kinds to build more advanced materials

3. Add node-based textures to the shaders

4. Create simple and complex materials, such as glass, stone, fire, and ice

Blender 2.5 HOTSHOT

ISBN: 978-1-84951-310-4   Paperback: 332 pages

Reclaiming Productivity for faster Java Web Development

1. Exciting projects covering many areas: modeling, shading, lighting, compositing, animation, and the game engine

2. Strong emphasis on techniques and methodology for the best approach to each project

3. Utilization of many of the tools available in Blender 3D for developing moderately complex projects

Please check **www.PacktPub.com** for information on our titles

CPSIA information can be obtained at www.ICGtesting.com
Printed in the USA
BVOW09s2125220315

392725BV00005BA/51/P